CHANGING PHILOLOGIES

Changing Philologies

Contributions to the Redefinition
of Foreign Language Studies
in the Age of Globalisation

edited by
Hans Lauge Hansen

Museum Tusculanum Press
University of Copenhagen
2002

Hans Lauge Hansen (ed.)
Changing Philologies
Contributions to the Redefinition
of Foreign Language Studies
in the Age of Globalisation

© Museum Tusculanum Press and the Authors 2002
Layout: Nils Soelberg
Cover design: Pernille Sys Hansen
Printed in Denmark by AKA Print, Aarhus
ISBN 87 7289 790 2

The editors gratefully acknowledge the financial support from
Landsdommer V. Gieses Legat
Sprogfagenes identitetsprojekt,
Det Humanistiske Fakultet, Københavns Universitet

Museum Tusculanum Press
University of Copenhagen
Njalsgade 92
DK-2300 København S
Danmark
www.mtp.dk

Contents

Introduction 7

The Challenge of the Traditional Foreign Language Studies
Susan Bassnett: Translation, Culture and History 15
Gert Sørensen: National Philology in a Globalized World 25
Anne Marie E. Jeppesen: Language as Intercultural Communication . 33
Hanne Leth Andersen: The Situation of the Foreign Language Studies.
  "Modern Language Studies in Current Educational Planning" ... 41

Philology and the Cultural Turn
Herbert Grabes: The Cultural Turn of Philology 51
Hans Lauge Hansen: A Change of Paradigm in Language Studies 63

Interdisciplinary Approaches
Jostein Børtnes: Lotman, Bakhtin, and the Problem of a Semiotics of
  Culture 77
Jacob L. Mey: The relation between Micro- and Macropragmatics in
  Modern Language Studies 89
Nigel Fabb: Complex Implied Form, Leisure Pursuits, and Cultural
  Studies 105

Translation – A Successful Meeting between Disciplines
Hanne Jansen: Translation Studies: From Linguistics and Beyond and
  Back Again 121
Lene Waage Petersen: Literary Translations between Philology and
  Aesthetics 137
Ingemai Larsen: Translation and Cultural History 151

Introduction

In our increasingly globalised world, the process of accelerated modernization sharpens the tensions within and between cultures at different levels. Within the centres, segments of non-contemporaneity are dissolved and traditional forms of collective social organization such as the family or trade unions lose weight, while in the so-called peripheries the core values of whole cultures undergo transformation. These processes are experienced ambivalently, both as a loss of traditional community values and as an increase in individual freedom. Economic and political globalisation reinforces international trade and communication, providing the conditions for increased mobility of populations. Concepts and strategies derived from the hegemonic discourses of economic and political power tend to invade all domains of civil society, and English spreads all over the planet as a corporate language or as a *lingua franca*, symbolizing on the one hand power and domination and on the other freedom and individuality. We have to acknowledge, in other words, that globalisation may promote world-wide democratisation and freedom from traditional autocratic regimes, as many western leaders are quick to stress; but it also produces conflicts and popular resistance associated with national, regional and local cultures. Cultural differences have taken over the role played by political and ideological differences during the cold war period, and cultural understanding has become a question of national security. This kind of culturally determined resistance is created in opposition to what is conceived of as the hegemonic discourses of the economic and political centres, and consequently always has a linguistic component. A Humanist approach to globalisation therefore presupposes highly developed linguistic competencies, while the widespread belief in English as the one sufficient tool only exacerbates the blind spot generated by economic and political globalisation theories.

In this situation, the humanities are faced at the turn of the millennium with the necessity of redefining themselves as a field of knowledge, and within this overall discussion what appears particularly pressing is the need to find a new role for modern language studies. Foreign language studies, both in Denmark and internationally, find themselves in a paradoxical situation: on the one hand, society is in great need of linguistic and cultural competencies, but on the other, foreign language departments at the universities are going through a slump: their student entries are declining, their academic prestige is waning and they are subjected to cutbacks in funding. What is the reason for this malaise? And what can be done about it? These were some of the fundamental questions behind the conference *Changing Philologies*, organised by the *Institute of Advanced Studies in the Humanities* and held in Copenhagen in February 2002. This book contains the proceedings from this conference in three of its four sections, with the last section appending three papers on the topic of Translation. The four sections are:

- The Challenge of Traditional Foreign Language Studies
- Philology and the Cultural Turn
- Interdisciplinary Approaches
- Translation – A Successful Meeting between Disciplines

The Challenge of Traditional Foreign Language Studies
In her paper "Translation, Culture and History" Professor **Susan Bassnett**, pro-Vice-Chancellor at the University of Warwick, raises a discussion on the role of western systems of education in the development of the present crisis in intercultural understanding, which culminated in the terrorist attack on September 11th, 2001 and the subsequent war in Afghanistan. According to Susan Bassnett, the western systems of education all share the same idealized belief in the progress of modernity, and for generations have disregarded the necessity of teaching children to understand and respect cultural differences in the form of the cultural, the linguistic and the historical "other". "Why bother with other languages when English is taking over the globe? Why bother with history when what matters is improving the present for the future?" (p. 15). In contrast to this imperialist view, Bassnett maintains that it is important to recognize that societies are vastly different from one another, and that those differences are enshrined in language. In order to overcome what she calls "this combination of monolingualism and amnesia", Bassnett proposes a number of new ways for teaching cultural differences that are not just appendages to the monolingual, future-oriented system. Among these is the strategy of cultural untranslatability. Here she suggests that language studies should interact more closely with a whole range of disciplines like anthropology, sociology, politics, economic and business studies in order to relate linguistic competencies to the complexities of today's world.

In "National Philology in a Globalised World" senior lecturer **Gert Sørensen** of the University of Copenhagen asks whether the traditional philological paradigm of national histories and literary canons and a linguistics based on national, unified languages, can function as an appropriate preparation for the challenge to the humanities posed by economic and political globalisation. According to Sørensen, the study of foreign languages has always been an activity related to the understanding of the

"Other", and the present-day tendencies of increased globalisation, dominated by the USA, must be comprehended in the light of a long history of colonialism, headed by the Mediterranean countries for centuries following the late Middle Ages. Discussing concepts like "the new Empire" of Hardt and Negri and "the clash of civilizations" of Samuel Huntington, Sørensen proposes that "a new philology of culture or of re-thinking language and culture as a joint venture in the age of globalisation presents one possible way of rearranging our specific knowledge" (p. 30).

The relation between languages and cultures will become an important field of investigation in the future, and the external conditions for an overall change of profile by foreign language departments towards a programme of studies and a line of investigation giving priority to this field are very favourable at the moment. It is one of the most important parameters within the cultural politics of the European Union, and a proposal from the departments of foreign language studies at the University of Copenhagen for a research programme grounded in an intercultural profile has had a very positive reception in the debate on the strategy for the Danish Research Council for the Humanities 2003 – 2007. It is up to us to decide whether to accept this challenge; but if we do, we must also accept the responsibility of making our professional expertise accessible and useful in other fields within the humanities, and in the rest of society. And the challenge is at least two-fold.

Firstly, foreign language studies must reflect theoretically upon the relation between such entities as language, culture, identity, history and the self-knowledge and imaginary world pictures represented in art and literature, as argued by senior lecturer **Anne Marie Jeppesen** from the University of Copenhagen. In her contribution, "Language as intercultural communication", Jeppesen criticises the traditional concepts of language and culture that for many years dominated foreign language studies; i.e. "language" understood as a closed system of relations and "culture" conceived of in the form of a national culture. Instead she advocates an intercultural approach to foreign language studies that gives priority to the study of language as an active instrument in the construction of cultural identities in a world of changing conditions (p. 38)

Secondly, our professional skills must be made visible and relevant. It is no longer enough to instruct our students in language and literature; it will be our responsibility to explain why foreign language acquisition is important, and to show how the study of literary and cultural issues is a part of an intercultural *Bildungs*-process for the individual student, as described by senior lecturer **Hanne Leth Andersen** of the University of Aarhus. In the article "The Situation of Modern Language Studies within Current Educational Planning", Andersen engages with the changes we have experienced over the last century and especially during the last decades. According to Andersen, important changes can be detected in the character of the knowledge that language studies aim at producing and in the competencies that students are expected to acquire. Where the knowledge-ideal of traditional philology was general and multi-focussed, modern language studies have been transformed by theoretical specialization. And where traditional philology focussed on the reading and interpretation of texts, modern language studies are committed to teaching communicative competencies. Given the changes in the concepts of "language" and "culture" mentioned above, Andersen proposes that the object of study of foreign language studies should be conceptualised as "language in its cultural and social context" (p. 50) and that we should apply the new theoretical approaches to the competencies which our students will require in their future employment, giving priority to such topics as communication, culture, intercultural communication, discourse analysis, rhetoric etc.

Philology and the Cultural Turn

It is necessary to accept that foreign language departments no longer function as traditional philological institutions investigating the correlation between history, culture, language and literature, and that in the light of this breakdown of the traditional philological paradigm the problematic identity of academic language studies must be subjected to discussion and analysis. In a number of areas, developments during the last three decades of the twentieth century have altered the academic landscape within humanistic learning. It will suffice to mention such factors as increased economic and political globalisation, the impact of information technology, the theoretical compartmentalisation of the humanistic sciences and the overall change in the professional profile of arts graduates, all of which must be considered when projecting reforms. As these factors are common to all foreign language departments, they invite an intensified interdisciplinary effort at all levels: internationally, nationally and locally. And collaboration is especially important in the present situation, which calls for a radical rethinking of some basic theoretical presuppositions and key concepts of the whole philological enterprise under the impression of a general Cultural Turn within the Humanities.

Professor **Herbert Grabes** of the University of Giessen discusses the future role of the philologies within what he calls the "new overarcing paradigm of *Kulturwissenschaften*" (p. 55). He suggests that the philological unity of various disciplines determined by a specific language continues to make sense, or makes sense anew, under the heading of Cultural Studies; but if the range of possible objects of investigation becomes almost unlimited within this line of study, it seems the more necessary to clearly limit the perspective under which the various features of culture are approached by philology. Grabes consequently points out a number of challenges that a new and theoretically self-reflexive philology should engage with. Firstly, he mentions the semiotic study of "recurrencies" within culture, understood as a complex text or web of signification; secondly, he deals with what he calls the cultural history of literature, i.e. the role of literature in the construction of cultural or national identity as an imaginary construct; and as a third issue he mentions "the history of the functions of literature", that might deal with issues related to the problem of representation and world-making in literary fiction compared to the same problem in non-fictional texts. This last area of study would examine uses of literary discourse in order to make visible the gap between ideological idealizations and the actual conditions and practices of life, thus fostering a critical stance (p. 59).

In the article "A Change of Paradigm in Language Studies", senior lecturer **Hans Lauge Hansen** of the University of Copenhagen proposes that the theoretical changes we have witnessed during the last decades of the 20th century may be conceived of as a general change in the epistemological paradigm, to use Foucault's expression, that abandons the anti-subjectivist modernist paradigm and paves the way for a new pragmatically oriented paradigm of dialogical thinking. According to this paradigm, the human sciences have an obligation to reflect upon themselves as activities that at one and the same time make a contribution to scientific knowledge about the world and contribute to the construction of their own object of investigation. Thus foreign language studies should engage in a thorough revision of all its disciplines, debating the conceptualisation of the relation between languages and cultures within each, and developing a variety of interdisciplinary approaches within what could be called a new philology of culture.

Interdisciplinary approaches

A real and profound change of paradigm in any field of knowledge should have the character of an interdisciplinary enterprise. Ties with existing scientific traditions and communities must be loosened in order to concentrate on the actual object of study from the perspective of other methods and traditions. We have chosen three approaches to this question, presented under the heading of "interdisciplinary approaches" by Professor Jostein Børtnes of the University of Bergen, Norway, Professor Emeritus Jacob Mey of the University of Southern Denmark, and Professor Nigel Fabb from the University of Strathclyde in Glasgow, Scotland.

In the article "Lotman, Bakhtin, and the Problem of a Semiotics of Culture", **Jostein Børtnes** defends the hypothesis that "the human sciences are not dealing with objects, but with other subjects" (p. 87). This point of view is based on Mikhail Bakhtin's approach to language, according to which no two speakers use language in exactly the same way and every utterance must be considered as a unique event. This means that language should not to be studied as an objective thing but must be conceived of as a living entity. The Norwegian professor therefore suggests that the relation between languages and cultures may be understood, using Lars Rodseth's biological metaphor, as an interactive community of populations of meanings.

Jacob Mey, whose point of departure is the split between traditional philology and analytical linguistics, takes us on a personal linguistic odyssey from early structuralism under the influence of Louis Hjelmslev to contemporary pragmatics. His remarkable conclusion is that the language studies have, so to speak, travelled full circle back to the philological interest in areas like history and culture: "The changing philologies of the late 20th century seem to have reverted to their origin: philology as the study of the entire human being" (p. 103).

Nigel Fabb closes this section of interdisciplinary approaches with his presentation of a study of complexity of form in both poetry and leisure pursuits. The linguistically based techniques with which he investigates aesthetic form in poetry reveal that the same kind of complexity invoked to account for the aesthetic experience in relation to poetry may also be found in all kinds of leisure pursuits such as bird-watching, gardening, hill walking and hiking.

Translation – A Successful Meeting between Disciplines
Finally, a new section on the perspectives of translation has been added to the conference-proceedings, containing three papers written by scholars from the Dept. of Romance Languages at the University of Copenhagen. They maintain that translation can be understood as something that goes between, connects, mediates or links the different disciplines of traditional language studies. And, as shown by Susan Bassnett, the concept of "translation" can be conceived of both as a concrete practice and as a metaphor for the cultural encounter. Understood as a practice, translation mediates between linguistics, literary studies, aesthetics and cultural studies because a translation cannot be successful if it focuses on only one of these dimensions. Understood as a metaphor, translation can be said to take place whenever we engage in a cultural encounter. The meaning of the words of a specific discourse must always be interpreted or created in dialogue with different cultural contexts, different frameworks and different value systems. In this sense, translation is a process mediating between different cultures.

The first of the three papers, "Translation Studies and Linguistics Revisited" by lecturer **Hanne Jansen,** gives a survey of the different theoretical trends within translation studies from the fifties up until today, from early formalist linguistic positions via the succeeding pragmatic and cultural turns to the recent revival of interest in empirical linguistic data within corpus-based translation studies. In her own approach to translation studies, Jansen takes her point of departure in her practical experience with translation, and defends a close and tangible meeting with language. Her work is with the significance of word classes in text and translation, where the framework provided by Cognitive Grammar has proved especially relevant in describing the semantics of word classes and the consequences of changes in their frequency and distribution, both on the texture of the text and on the mental images evoked - aspects closely related to the text-typological considerations crucial to the act of translation.

In the paper called "Literary Translation between Philology and Aesthetics", senior lecturer **Lene Waage Petersen** discusses the problems related to the translation of aesthetically elaborated texts after the hermeneutic turn of literary studies. Following the phenomenological discrimination between the textual form and the process of reading, Petersen considers the description of the different levels of signification in their relation to the aesthetic experience. Applying Christopher Collins' concepts of enactive and critical interpretation, Petersen concludes that the translation of a literary text is not comparable to a musician's playing from a score, an image often used to describe the reader's actualisation of textual meaning, but must be regarded as the creation of a new score, open for new enactive readings by other readers.

In the concluding paper, entitled "Translation and Cultural History", lecturer **Inge Merete Larsen** applies her knowledge of literary practices in the former Portuguese colonies in Africa in engaging with the complex question of the translation of texts written in postcolonial contexts or texts written in minor languages. In both cases, she suggests, the fact that words cannot be translated adequately if they are separated from their cultural and historical setting indicates that the translator should have rich cultural and historical knowledge in order to be able to understand and recreate the textual meaning. What Larsen calls the "egalitarian view on languages" that has prevailed in many translation theories turns out to be inadequate in a postcolonial context and in relation to minor languages, because these languages are subjected to asymmetrical power relations (p. 156). A profound knowledge of the history of culture is called for, which, according to Larsen, extends from an understanding of morphology and syntax via familiarity with the traditions of literary genres to knowledge of the general lines of world history. And the paper concludes with the assertion that the multidisciplinary approach that that has proved to be necessary for the development of translation studies in a globalised world, coincides with the ideal and *raison d'être* of foreign language departments.

Translation, Culture, and History

by

Susan Bassnett

University of Warwick

To say that the world has changed irrevocably since September 11th is almost a cliche. It has been said endlessly, and speculation about the far-reaching effect of the changes fills the pages of newspapers. Yet one important aspect of the tragic clash between different views seems to have been overlooked: the role of western systems of education in contributing to the present crisis, and the absence of any clear way forward that will help the next generation to move on.

The British, US and European systems of education are very different on the surface, but all share a similar set of values. Belief in democracy, in the rights of the individual, in free speech and freedom of information are fundamental. Implicit in all this is a belief in progress, an idealized view of the world that sees society as always moving forward, always improving on what has gone before. "Things can only get better" was the Labour Party campaign song of 1997, echoing the language of advertising where everything is always new, improved and better than ever. Countless politicians in Europe and North America recite similar slogans. Across the Atlantic, the idea of continual improvement lies at the heart of the American dream. Generations of immigrants arrived in the United States with a desire to progress, to go beyond what they had left behind, to move forward, to become Americans.

Becoming American has meant shedding the skin of the past, learning a new language, turning one's back on history. Significantly the teaching of history and the teaching of languages are both low priorities in the US school system. Why bother with other languages when English is taking over the globe? Why bother with history when what matters is improving the present for the future? In Britain, a parallel process is also taking place: history makes contemporary post-devolution Britain uncomfortable, for it is a history of the expansion of an empire and, more recently, the loss of an empire, a difficult history to come to terms with in an increasingly multi-cultural society. The difficulty that so many British people have with the very terminology of 'Britain' and 'Britishness' highlights this. Yet, when we cross the Channel and drive in the rest of Europe, our vehicles still bear the initials GB, for Great Britain.

History in British schools is taught in chunks, and these days appears to consist of either the Tudors or the Second World War, repeated at several points in a child's school career. My children have no chronological map in their heads at all, and despite GCSE and A level history their grasp of the past is thin. They have no idea of the importance of Afghanistan throughout the 19th century, for example. They are as ignorant of the long, complex relationship between Britain, Russia, India and Afghanistan as Afghan children are of what life is like in the United States. The Great Game might as well be the latest Nintendo title.

Foreign language learning in the UK today is almost as irrelevant. Modern languages in schools are in crisis. Fewer students opt for modern languages at university, and the recent Green Paper on reforming education contains plans to reduce the teaching of foreign languages in schools to merely 3 years from age 11 to 14. True, there is the stated intention to introduce language teaching in primary schools from the age of 7, but that is scheduled to start in 2012 and before it happens, a whole generation of teachers has to be recruited and trained, in a climate in which it is increasingly difficult to persuade anyone to enter teaching as a profession. We have produced in Britain a generation that cannot access other cultures except via translators and cannot access the past that has shaped the world they live in. All the chatter about multiculturalism is nothing more than a frail and patronizing attempt to compensate for the lack of interest in other cultural systems, for the failure of the education system to teach modern languages adequately and for the abandonment of anything but the most facile idea of history.

This combination of monolingualism and amnesia has dangerous consequences. If we set progress as an ideal goal, we will be contemptuous of those who hold on tightly to the past – witness Northern Ireland. If we do not value history, we will be unable to take seriously those who see the past as important enough to die for – witness the Balkans. If we see rationality and not faith as the cornerstone of society, then we will not take seriously those who are motivated by religious beliefs – witness what is happening now across the Islamic world and what happened after the collapse of communism. Above all, if we persist in training children to believe that there is a single universal model, that people are all the same really, just a little bit different in terms of customs and traditions from ourselves, we risk the kind of hubris that may kill many more thousands of innocent people.

It is important to recognize that societies are vastly different from one another, and those differences are enshrined in language. Arguably, languages are so different that no two cultures can ever share common ground. This, of course, is the Sapir-Whorf hypothesis, which invites us to consider that the worlds in which different societies live are distinct worlds, not the same world with different labels attached. In contrast to this hypothesis is the imperialist notion which we see time and again reflected in very diverse contexts which repudiates any idea of difference and rather demands acceptance of some (always the dominant culture's) idea of universality. We have seen this process in the founding of the Spanish colonies in the Americas, the British global empire, the Soviet absorption of the Baltic states and central European nations, not to mention Central Asia and today we see it in the United States' belief in American values as universal ones.

But difference, which the Western world has sought to play down, needs rather to be accentuated in our educational systems. We need to make children understand that not everyone, everywhere thinks as we do and, most importantly, often has no desire to think like us. We need also to make them understand that acknowledging difference does not mean that we should compromise our own beliefs. This applies as much to the past as to the present. We live at a time when history is constantly being reshaped to fit in with our current values, despite the obvious evidence that the past was different. How much paper has been wasted by people trying to prove that Shakespeare and Marlowe were not anti-semitic when they created Shylock or the Jew of Malta, when what is really needed is a clear explanation of why people thought in that way in the 16th century? Marina Warner, speaking on Radio 4 on the *Start the Week* the other day was expressing her concern about what she sees as the highly ambiguous implications of politicians apologizing for the past. If an apology is intended to be part of a genuine process of confession, acknowledgement and learning, she argues, what is the meaning of a contemporary politician apologizing for actions committed centuries ago in an age when those actions were not believed to have been sinful ones?

In our attempts to rewrite history to suit the politically correct, universalist notions of today we erase difference and reconceptualize the world of the past in our own image. Robert Darnton in his marvellous book, *The Great Cat Massacre, and other episodes in French Cultural History* outlines the reasons why an historian should recognize the significance of difference:

> ... other people are other. They do not think the way we do. And if we want to understand their way of thinking, we should set out with the idea of capturing otherness. Translated into the terms of the historian's craft, that may merely sound like the familiar injunction against anachronism. It is worth repeating, nonetheless; for nothing is easier than to slip into the comfortable assumption

> that Europeans thought and felt two hundred years ago just as we do today-allowing for the wigs and wooden shoes. We constantly need to be shaken out of a false sense of familiarity with the past to be administered doses of culture shock. (Darnton 1985; 4)

Darnton's thesis can be equally applicable in the study of other cultures, for those cultures are not merely mirror images of our own with different labels. Obviously there are basic biological similarities, but societies are structured in terms of systems of morality, ethics, aesthetics, politics and religion very, very differently and all those societies have different histories that have featured in making them what they are.

Some cultures have moved in the opposite direction to the West and have chosen to highlight difference. We do not seem to have understood that process at all, and indeed, we are uneasy and often contemptuous of it. Societies that stress gender difference through dress codes, for example, are regarded in the West as highly suspect. Once again, let us return to Afghanistan, and to the particular example of the wearing of the Afghan version of the veil, the burqua. The wives of the President of the United States and the British Prime Minister have both spoken out against the veil, and periodically this recurs in western feminist discourse. But the veiling of women is extraordinarily complex and varies according to place, class, age, status etc. To perceive the veil as a simplistic example of the opression of women is to misunderstand, it is to read the conventions of other cultures through our own conventions. And, of course, covering the head was common practice also in Europe until only a few decades ago and relics of that still remain – at weddings, for example, where hats are worn, or at ceremonial occasions, such as meeting the Queen at Buckingham Palace garden parties when hats are compulsory.

An example of the abyss that separates Western consciousness from that of other cultures can be seen in the attempt to offer aid to starving Afghan families in the autumn of 2001. Food parcels were parachuted in to war-ravaged destitute areas in the mountains when the aid crisis became more acute. But those parcels did not contain the kind of food the locals would have recognized. They were prepared for western palates, and, included such items as peanut butter and, with US attitudes to hygiene in mind, moist towlettes. This misguided attempt at aid reveals a great gulf in cultural understanding: the assumption is that not only will American food be enjoyed all over the world, but that it will be immediately recognized as food. What is demonstrated by this example is inadequate cultural knowledge.

The latter decades of the 20th century saw the rise of global English. Everyone now wants to learn English, the new *lingua franca* of the world. But the spread of global English has all kinds of consequences. For a start, more and more people become bi-lingual or multi-lingual, while native

English speakers become more isolated through their monolingualism. The international terrorist network that we view with such horror is indeed international, operating in many languages and blending into other cultures so well as to be able to hone in on the most vulnerable targets. How many people have the UK and US trained who could even begin to exercise similar understanding of other cultures and integrate into them to the point of invisibility? The absence of intercultural awareness programmes and degrees in cultural diplomacy says it all. All you need to succeed in the world today is English and a belief in Anglo-Saxon values; or rather, that is all you needed before September 11th 2001.

We need to find ways of teaching students about cultural difference that are not just add-ons to a monolingual, future-oriented system. This does not mean setting aside those aspects of our world that we believe are important. It means proclaiming those elements that we believe to be of significance, while at the same time taking seriously other systems and respecting them even though we may not approve of them. The Anglo-Saxon world has tended to dismiss anyone with strong religious views as fanatical, barbaric, primitive – the language used exposes our contempt, and reveals how we believe our rationalist system is inherently better. Yet instead of turning our backs on the so-called primitives, and pretending they are not there, we need to invest wholesale in trying to understand why so many millions of people find what they offer so attractive. We have invested minimally in understanding other cultures, so it is hardly surprising that now we find ourselves mystified by what is happening around us. Yet not so long ago, there were hundreds of thousands of British citizens competent in other languages and able to offer expert advice on other cultures. As they have died out, we have not bothered to replace them.

Let us now move from polemics to a consideration of possible future strategies to deal with some of these problems. Just before embarking on this discussion, however, let me introduce a brief autobiographical element. I currently hold a Chair in Comparative Literature, I founded the Centre for Translation and Comparative Cultural Studies at the University of Warwick, but the first position I held in a British university was as a Lecturer in Anglo-Saxon. I have moved, therefore, from a training that was totally classical, with Latin through my second year of university, a degree that was 60% Germanic philology, to cultural studies. Nor have I undergone a Pauline conversion on the road, because the subjects I enjoyed most as a student were Latin and Anglo-Saxon. I loved them because they enabled me to understand structures of language, to explain anomalies, to make sense of my linguistic maps. Contemporary cultural studies therefore connect unproblematically with Anglo-Saxon and the study of classical languages.

Equally though, I very soon saw that my passion was not shared by my students. Forced to study Anglo-Saxon in the second year of their degree course at the university where I was employed, the students hated every minute. So a solution had to be found, and what I discovered was what might loosely be described as a cultural approach. I threw away the syllabus and set up projects instead. Some of the students did projects on place names, the north of England being particularly rich in Saxon, Danish and Norwegian names, some did projects on surnames. We toured the countryside looking at Anglo-Saxon stone crosses and hog-backed stones, and investigated Norse influence on stone carving. When we turned to the epic, students compared the figure of a hero such as Beowulf to heroes in the Captain Marvel comics, and we listened to rap poets such as Linton Kwesi Johnson or punk poets such as John Cooper Clarke so that students would have an idea of what rhythmic poetry might sound like. Nor was this method of approaching Anglo-Saxon, as a senior philologist who despised my methods said, populist rubbish, (today he would have said 'dumbing-down') because through the year they learned a lot of Anglo-Saxon and a lot of Anglo-Saxon history. They also learned about the invention of Anglo-Saxon philology in the 19th century and the way in which the Germanic world came to be reinterpreted in the light of British imperial ambitions. As Southern Europe came increasingly in the post-Romantic period to be feminized, so Northern Europe, home of the Saxons and the Vikings was seen as the true inheritor of the best of Hellenic and Roman civilization. The average English schoolboy of the 1870s would have learned that the soft, sissified French and Italians had lost the plot a long time ago, corrupted by warm weather, too much wine, and Catholicism. Even the Renaissance collapsed in a maelstrom of corruption and decadence and had to be revivified by Northern Europeans. To study Anglo-Saxon meant therefore not only learning the language that had been the protoype of contemporary English, it meant also learning about the essence of Englishness, as constructed at the height of Empire. Students were invited to think about all that as well, to think about how the study of a dead language could have such profound political implications for contemporary society.

Over the years, having to rethink my assumptions about the role of philology and the teaching of languages has not been easy. I learned, as many of you will have done, via the old grammar and rote learning method. My children learn languages through the conversational method. The latter replaced the former, and practitioners of the communicative approach are often vehement in their repudiation of the older method. Yet in that repudiation, the baby appears to have been thrown out with the bathwater. In consequence, I find both methods equally flawed, though in different ways. I studied pages of verbs and declensions and rarely spoke a sentence. My children parrot phrases and have no sense of structure. Once they diverge from the scenario they have been studying, they are lost. Every time I write an article in the national press about this in the UK, I am deluged with letters from desperate teachers saying yes, we agree what can we do? How can we stem the tide? Should we try to teach grammar again? Should we punish grammatical errors? A few days ago Nottingham City Council declared that they would introduce a fine of £1 for every misuse of an apostrophe by a Council employee. As though the demise of the apostrophe can be halted! As though language were not dynamic and in a constant process of change! Can you stem the tide?

Of course, you can't. King Cnut famously sat at the edge of the sea and regally ordered the waves not to encroach on his royal presence and got his gown wet. We cannot go back to a grammar based method of teaching languages, because students are not trained to think in such a way. They are trained now to think in snapshots, and to make sense of fragments. They are not trained to think in the old structures. So our starting point must be to help them make links between the snapshots and to enable them to make informed choices.

Some framework is essential. Call it grammar if you like, but a framework of sorts is necessary, and it needs flagging up as a framework from the outset. Sneaking bits of grammar in through the back door, particularly if done in one of the lavishly illustrated over-crowded textbooks that students use these days is pretty useless. But some grammar needs to be taught not just for its own sake, but for what it does and what it can do. Ironically, the sort of courses for which badly taught adults pay good money (improve your English skills etc) do precisely this: they explain that which was not explained much earlier. If grammar were taught as part of a transferrable skills package, with its objectives clearly articulated, students might be more receptive to it. And if they were also taught about where the rules of grammar came from, and about how they operate differently in different languages, that would give a few more snapshots for them to link in a chain.

Cultural difference needs to be foregrounded. It is useless teaching conversations that you would never have in another culture. I start every year my MA in Translation Studies with a set of elementary examples of cultural untranslatability. One such example involves the different codes of acceptability socially when talking about health matters: it is perfectly proper in some cultures to discuss one's medical condition, while in others it is unacceptably rude. Another example involves the English obsession with 'please' and 'sorry' which appears so bizarre to non-native speakers. Yet another example considers the different greetings systems that operate in English and French, where the day is divided into a tripartite structure in English (Good morning, Good afternoon and Good evening) with only two greetings in French (Bonjour/Bonsoir). As a second stage to the exercise, we consider the shifts in social register as the day proceeds, so that the greeting 'Good evening' is a much higher register than 'Good morning', a fact which reflects patterns of social behaviour when the greeting system was bedding down in the language. These elementary examples enable us to establish the inadequacy of concepts of equivalence, to consider the implications of even the seemingly most straightforward act of translation and to think hard about the processes of negotiation and mediation that take place as we shift from one language to another.

The role of translation in language learning is crucial and has been used abominably. Translation involves all kinds of complex stages yet has tended to be used merely as a device for assessing linguistic competence. Pushing students to think about the limits of translatability is an excellent and challenging exercise in which to engage. Bad translations are excellent as a means of engaging students' interest, as is the process of back translation which enables the process of linguistic transfer to be seen clearly.

Translation seen at its broadest in terms of culture as well as language has a vital role to play. It is important here to remember that though language learning may be in decline, cultural awareness training is a huge international growth industry. Business people need to know about other cultures, they need to know all kinds of things – about appropriate verbal and non-verbal communication, about proxemics, about status, about the significance of factors such as gender or age, about politeness strategies, they need to know how time-keeping and deadlines are seen in different cultures, whether business deals take place in meetings or outside, whether individual decision-making is recognized or discouraged. In short, they need to know about cultural difference, and so we come round in a circle to our starting point, where it was suggested that the shock of September 11th 2001 was compounded by the fact that western educational systems had failed to prepare citizens adequately to deal with what was, effectively, the clash between two diametrically opposite world views.

Language studies need to interact more closely with cultural anthropology, with business studies, with sociology, politics, economics, in short, with a whole range of disciplines that hitherto have had an uneasy relationship with one another. Nobody is going to return to the difficult task of learning another language – and it is much more difficult than those subjects which students can take up and set down at any point, without having to acquire a baseline of competence upon which to build- unless there is a clear purpose. That purpose, it can be argued, is to understand more about the complexities of today's world, a world in which millions of people are in transit, millions are multilingual, moving between languages, and millions are dispossessed and seeking an identity. The great danger for

Europe is that we turn inwards, at a time when we should be doing the opposite and looking outwards.

We need also to ensure that language study is based in the present but firmly rooted in the past. Understanding your own past is a means of moving forward into the future with a better chance of not repeating mistakes. If we train generations with no idea of their own history, no sense of how things came to be, no notion of why they speak as they do and how their own language has been shaped, no idea of why children in some countries are taught to hate as soon as they can walk, they will have no chance of changing anything.

The brilliant children's author, Philip Pullman, recently became the first children's writer to win the Whitbread Prize for his novel, third in a trilogy, *The Amber Spyglass*. This extraordinary saga told through three long novels has defied all prediction about what children read today, just as the Harry Potter books have done. Both J. K. Rowling and Philip Pullman write long books (educationalists have been telling us for some time now that children will only read short books) they write difficult books in terms of language, style and plot, books that are not politically correct or about today's social problems. They have written books that are about intercultural and intertemporal understanding, about the eternal struggle between good and evil that can only be won through hard work, sacrifice, understanding the past and trusting in the future. Pullman's protagonists set themselves the seemingly impossible task of building the Republic of Heaven; surely Humanities educators should aspire to nothing less? This is an ideal time for philologists and for teachers in the Humanities generally to follow such a lead and boldly go out to work with the next generation in genuinely new, challenging ways. What we need to change are the structures within which we work, for in effecting such changes the Humanities can be defended as central to social and intellectual development everywhere.

References

Bassnett, Susan: 2002. *Translation Studies* (3rd Revised ed.). London and New York, Routledge.

Bassnett Susan and André Lefevere: 1998. *Constructing Cultures*. Clevedon, Multilingual Matters.

Darnton, Robert: 1985. *The Great Cat Massacre, and Other Episodes in French Cultural History.* New York, Vintage.

Sapir, Edward: 1956. *Culture, Language and Personality*. Berkeley, Los Angeles, University of California Press.

Pullman, Philip: 2002. *The Amber Spyglass*. London, Scolastic.

National Philology in a Globalized World

by

Gert Sørensen

University of Copenhagen

Studying foreign languages in a small country like Denmark has always had the aspect of making the country a little more broadminded. In the 18th century the most spoken languages among the élites were French and German. Since World War II English, or some sort of, has taken over as the most important foreign language, now shared by the entire population through the education system. However, with the final building of the Danish nation-state after the defeat to the Germans in 1864 the knowledge of languages also meant an increasing understanding of the differencies between homeland and those outside. Thus, studying foreign languages, today, intensifies our understanding of historical stratifications and hierarchies among nation-states, each of which is positioned within what Wallerstein years ago called the world-system (Wallerstein 1990, pp. 157-71). You might even define the person skilled in language as a spy or a mediator, who from conversations with foreigners and based of his or her insight into their cultures has something to tell us about foreign peoples and their ways of thinking, of acting, and of prospecting the future in order to make what is 'out there' lesser unpredictable.

I suggest that this activity of understanding the Otherness, although not fully exploited, is crucial to our work by making us capable of grasping at least some aspects of the ongoing globalization. With the emergence of a new global market-place and of an entire new world order of financial and political power, no doubt, globalization is on the agenda. According to Giddens: "Every business guru talks about it. No political speech is complete without reference to it" (Giddens 1999, p. 7). Whether you like it or not, the word globalization pushes itself forward and has become a new keyword for us, too, in as much as the global processes have had a determinant impact on national languages and cultures, which until now have constituted the somewhat unproblematic objects of our teaching and research.

However, divided between those, responsible for language-learning and grammar, those, responsible for literature, and finally those, responsible for history or cultural history, one might ask: are we sufficiently prepared to take on our role in constructing the general intellect in the sense of what Hardt and Negri in their recent book have called "a collective, social intelligence created by accumulated knowledge, techniques, and know-how" (Hardt & Negri 2000, p. 364). Of course, being in a defensive position, the boundaries between regarding globalization as a threat or as a challenge are almost non existent. The feeling of threat can, no doubt, be explained by the fact that theories about globalization have mostly been advanced within a sociological or politological discourse on international relations, that is outside the 'soft' humanities, although issues concerning postnationality, postcolonialism, the Americanization of culture, postmodern identities following the increasing geographical and social mobility of individuals and of entire groups of populations are all phenomena to be seen in well-known linguistic and cultural manifestations.

Thus, as teachers and researchers we cannot isolate ourselves from a globalized world. But we can discuss and choose our scientific attitude to the new world order. And we have to turn our attention to the velocity of the continuous upgrading or downgrading of knowledge, not to mention the levelling of linguistic and cultural diversity made by mass-culture in combination with the expanding media. Parts of traditional academic knowledge are disappearing or have been displaced, because we don't have the conceptual or the institutional capabilities to reproduce them or because of indifference or simply outdating.

Due to the growth of high-grade qualifications and of outside research-centres as a result of private investments and public priorities, the universities no longer have their former monopoly of knowledge. However, as opposed to other sorts of knowledge-production, the departments of human sciences have a responsibility to maintain a long-term collective memory of the past as a distinctive and integrated feature of the present and of the future, too. Humanities accentuate the model of what might be called slowscience (analogous to slowfood) rejecting any attempt to reduce knowledge to information, hastily produced by dominant systems of communication.

It is generally believed that the phenomenon of globalization is of a more recent date and popped up mainly due to the fact that the US is now the only global power, thus favouring the global status of English as the Language of Wider Communication.

But long before the language of globalization became English beginning with the expansion of Britain as the workshop of the world in the 19th century, taken over by the Americans in the 20th century, the states of Southern Europe (Portugal, Spain and later on France) had already acted in global terms and conceptualized their building of world-wide empires. A long history of clashes of cultures and civilizations and of mutual acculturations as well is catalogued in libraries of texts (Ginzburg 1999, pp. 71-91), not to mention the conflicts and intercultural relations between or within the single European states. And it is a history that continues, until the collapse of these empires in the 19th and the 20th centuries forced a reshaping of national identities in the European mother countries and in their former colonies as well. This briefly outlined history is an integrated part of our accumulated knowledge or ought to be so to an even greater extent by including – to give an example – not only Spanish and Portuguese speaking Latin-America but the French and Portuguese speaking areas in Africa as well. It is not enough – studying, let's say, French – to focus on France in the traditional sense of a well-defined territory and a well-defined language.

Thus, Romance-speaking Europe within and outside Europe has had its share in constructing the globally dominant Western civilization, although its single states have had their own specific history within the general history of European civilization. Let me point out the change of relative strength between France and Britain in the period of the Napoleonic wars, followed by the French defeat in the war with Germany in 1870-71. After that humiliation of national Grandeur French intellectuals, such as Ernest Rénan and Émile Durkheim and later on Raymond Aron, felt the need for a rebirth of French culture suggesting further assimilation to the models of German culture.

According to Hardt and Negri the distinctive features of what they see as an ongoing construction of a new Empire are: 1) Its rule have no limits and no territorial boundaries limit its reign; 2) It does not present itself as former imperialistic states originating in conquest; 3) It not only regulates human interactions but also seeks to rule over human nature in the sense of what Foucault called biopolitics; 4) It is dedicated to the eternal peace, although it is "bathed in blood" (Hardt & Negri 2000, pp. xiv-v). And to sum up: "[S]overeignty has taken a new form, composed of a series of national and supranational organisms united under a single logic of rule. This new global form of sovereignty is what we call Empire" (Ibid., p. xii). This is what we have to relate to, and to push it to extremes: world-order before nation-order – a Copernican turn not without consequences for our way of organizing teaching and research.

In his famous book on the clashes of civilizations, Samuel Huntington gives a somewhat less homogeneous picture of a rather complex globalizationprocess. As an exponent of dominant politological discourse on globalization his introduction of a civilizational paradigm (Huntington 1998, pp. 36-39) is interesting to us, in so far as it makes a breach in his own dominant discourse, which he – in my opinion – is not able to implement fully with his conceptual device. The question is: are we only to deliver a supplement or are we in a position to re-think the whole issue – and if so, on what ground? I don't have the complete answer. If anyone has. But our linguistic and hermeneutic, and I might add historicistic approach, gives us at least some tools for a better understanding not only of what is different but also and of what is submitted to change.

Huntington marks out four scenarios that have often been taken into account in the period after the fall of the Berlin-wall: 1) the world is becoming one world; 2) the world will be divided between us and them (McWorld versus Jihad) (Barber 1995); 3) a world of more or less sovereign states (the Westphalean model of traditional realistic power-politics); 4) a world of chaos, characterized by the collapse of state-structures and the emergence of new regional and supranational entities (Huntington 1998, pp. 31-35). However, Huntington points at a fifth scenario. Not that the scenarios already mentioned do not contain some elements of truth, easily to be verified on subaltern levels of a rather complex and stratified process of globalization. But what he intends to introduce is a new civilizational paradigm with reference to 8-9 different civilizations (Western, African, Islamic, Sinic, Japanese, Orthodox, Hindu, Buddhist, Latin American, and among which the Western civilization is only one and in the long run not even the fittest).

Of importance for us – obviously to be explored in more depth – is the use, Huntington makes of the French historian Fernand Braudel (Braudel 1980), who in his writings underscores the following distinctive aspects of a civilization: a civilization forms a unitary culture; it often consists of different languages; although each civilization – as history has taught – passes through a period of origin and of consolidation, and finally of decline, to be classified as such a civilization cannot be without long-term social and cultural capabilities. In spite of the fact that it is submitted to change, a civilization has to show a certain stability over time. This is, what Braudel meant when introducing his famous thesis on la longue durée of historical phenomena. Furthermore, Huntington focuses on what happens when two civilizations clash, that is when one is dominant (as Western civilization) and the other is lesser dominating or even dominated. Apart from the possibilities of armed conflicts, Huntington lines up different types of negative reaction or of hybridized combinations (Huntington 1998, pp. 72-74): 1) rejectionism (i.e. militant groups of Islam; or the 'Movimiento Civil Zapatista' in Mexico, an example of a resistance identity, according to Manuel Castells (Castells 2001, p. 8, pp. 63-81)); 2) Kemalism (Kemal Atatürk's full-scale modernization of Turkey); and 3) reformism (China's introduction of market-economy without taking over Western values of democracy and pluralism).

However, our reading of European state-based civilization has shown us a high degree of internal conflicts and warfare combined with the flow of cultural and intellectual elements across the ever-shifting borders. Until the long European civilwar (1914-1945) this was the model that mostly favoured the building of the great European powers and their imperialistic structures. In the words of Immanuel Wallerstein we might say that the existence itself of European nation-states is due to that very same world-system of conflicts, self-assertion and reciprocal recognitions, that the European states themselves, in different moments and with different weight and outcome, have formed (Wallerstein 1990, p. 165). No French language and culture without the strong centralistic French state. And no French state of that dimension and of that intrinsic power, without ambitious geopolitical strategies culminating in the period of the great revolution and the Napoleonic wars (Brunot 1967), and to be continued throughout the 19th century. Today the same world-system deprives the nation-states of their historical identities and rearranges the former hierarchies among the world's languages and cultures. If we are not aware of this fact, imprisoned as we often are, each of us in his or her national philoloughy, we might not even take notice of what is happening on larger scales, although we cannot avoid the consequences.

In this respect politics (world-politics), languages and cultures cannot be separated, indeed languages and narrative settings of reality are the main sources to explore the continuous affirmations or weakings or even denials of the hegemonic and interpellative state-structures. Language and culture make up the 'inner side' of the state. Through language and culture individuals get familiar with power, or they experience their own positions and possibilities as well within these structures of power. It is through language and culture that individuals in this period of globalization acquire knowledge about the crisis of the nation-state as one imagined community and its transformation to an intercultural rather than multicultural community.

Samuel Huntington is, indeed, one fine example of an IP-theorist who with his civilizational paradigm shows us an open-minded approach toward phenomena of language and culture motivated by his need to better understand the elements of continuities, of breakdowns and of decays that constitute a civilization and its historicity. Bob Jessop, a neo-gramscian political scientist from the University of Lancaster, just to give one more example of the actual reassessment of theories on globalization, he, too, turns his attention to critical analysis of discourse and to narrative theory as well (Jessop 1999a). My point is that we – with our philological traditions of linguistic and cultural studies – are in possession of even more detailed sets of theories compared to political science. Without our joint efforts of close ups and long shots – to make use of the metaphors of the Italian microhistorian Carlo Ginzburg (Ginzburg 1994, p. 526) – rational knowledge of the globalized world would lack in richness.

Competitiveness is, certainly, a favourite word of currently dominant neoliberal discourse, which has already found its way into the world of universities now submitted to the mania of benchmarking, of ranking, and of management-inspired leadership and budgeting. That is why we have to relate to this verified reality, simply because the whole issue of competitive positions reflects the increasing loss of autonomous decision-making that the universities and in a wider context nation-states, too, are going through at this time. The welfare-state has been forced to some extent to abandon or at least diminish the dimensions of the former politics of public services based on criteria which were not dictated by the norms of market-economy. Today the welfare-state is taking the form of what has been called the competition State. The state as a decommodifying agent has been reshaped becoming now a commodifying agent of privatisation or better reprivatisation and reallocation of economic and intellectual resources as well (Cerny 1990, p. 230).

Competitiveness has often been conceived of in purely economic terms of profitability. Bob Jessop points out one main contradiction, today, between short-sighted economic rationality and what he sees as the real dynamics of competition, deeply rooted in value-resources such as qualifying knowledge and trust, which need years or decades to be build up. To Jessop, it is one thing to look at economy as a space only for exchange of commodities, and quite another thing to analyse economy as embedded in a system of economic and non-economic capabilities and competences (Jessop 1999b). Facing continuous cutbacks in the field of sciences and higher education, although this country does not show any sign of economic crisis at all, one might ask, if such politics do not, in fact, weaken our competitiveness in the long run. On the other hand our knowledge of foreign language and culture as a kind of 'soft' intellectual capital slowly accumulated over the centuries might leave us – as Danes – with some further liberty of action and of forecasting possible future scenarios in a globalized world of competition and of cultural take-overs as well.

Thus, in a complex world of proliferations of new stratified and ever-changing identities, where nothing can be taken for granted any longer, we have to ask ourselves, if our divided sections of nation-based linguistics, literature and cultural studies are adequate to assure our survival as independent departments. A new philology of culture or of re-thinking language and culture as a joint venture in the age of globalization presents one possible way of rearranging our specific knowledge. Apart from the many questions it brings up, indeed, it expresses a more offensive approach to our problems of lacking incisiveness in society. Furthermore, this impression, to my mind, is confirmed by its epistemological and ontological rootedness in what is commonly known as the linguistic and hermeneutic turn. If so, a new philology of culture gives us some tools to understand what Karl Polanyi in 1944 called the great tranformation with reference to the emergence of modern mass-society and its new forms of subjectivity. And we might add that this is also the period of Europe's loss of its centrality following the process of decolonization and of the emergence of new voices, which claimed and still claim to be heard and understood on their own terms. A language-based knowledge of cultural identities and changes is what we can offer in order to understand the unpredictable Otherness better, in combination with actual redefinitions of ourselves as Danes, Europeans, and world-citizens at the same time.

References

Barber, B.R.: 1995. *Jihad vs. McWorld*. New York, Times Books.

Braudel, Fernand: 1980. *On History*. Chicago, University of Chicago Press.

Brunot, F.: 1967. *Histoire de la langue française des origines à nos jours*. Tome IX. Partie 1: Le français, langue nationale; Partie 2: Les événements, les institutions et la langue (nouv. ed.). Paris, Librairie Armand Colin.

Castells, Manuel: 2001. *The Information Age. Economy, Society and Culture*. Vol. II. *Power of Identity*. Oxford, Blackwell Publishers (1997).

Cerny, Philip G.: 1990. *The Changing Architecture of Politics. Structure, Agency, and the Future of the State*. London-New Delhi, SAGE Publications.

Giddens, Anthony: 1999. *Runaway World. How Globalization is reshaping our lives*. London, Profile Books.

Ginzburg, Carlo: 1994. "Microstoria: due o tre cose che so di lei", *Quaderni Storici* n.86, aug.

- 1999 "Alien Voices. The Dialogic Element in Early Modern Jesuit Historiography". *History, Rhetoric, and Proof. The Menahem Stern Jerusalem Lectures*. Hanover-London, University Press of New England.

Hardt, Michael & Negri, Antonio: 2000. *Empire*. Cambridge (Mass.)-London, Harvard University Press.

Huntington, Samuel P.: 1998. *The Clash of Civilizations and the Remaking of World Order* (1996). London et al., Touchstone Books.

Jessop, Bob: 1999a. "Narrating the Future of the National Economy and the National State? Remarks on Remapping Regulation and Reinventing Governance". G. Steinmetz (ed.), *State/Culture: State Formation after the Cultural Turn*. Ithaca, Cornell University Press
  (www.comp.lancs.ac.uk/sociology/soc014rj.html).

- 1999b. "Reflections on Globalization and its (Il)logics". P. Dicken et al. (eds.), *Globalization and the Asia Pacific. Contested Territories*. London, Routledge (www.comp.lancs.ac.uk/sociology/soc013rj.html).

Polanyi, Karl: 1944. *The Great Transformation*. New York, Holt, Rinehart & Winston.

Wallerstein, Immanuel: 1990. "Societal Development, or Development of the World-System?". M. Albow & E. King (eds.), *Globalization, Knowledge and Society*. London-New Delhi, SAGE Publications.

Language as Intercultural Communication

by

Anne Marie E. Jeppesen

University of Copenhagen

1. The present split between our disciplines and how it came about

In the foreign language departments we talk about a split between three areas in teaching and research: language, literature, and history/culture. The former two have been core disciplines since the beginning of the existence of the language departments but during the past decade or more the latter has begun to play a more significant role. In this paper I am going to argue in favour of a furtherance of collaboration between these different fields.

The study of grammar and language are still, as is to be expected, core disciplines, but mostly separated from the more communicative parts of the programs, as well as from literature and the history or culture of the different countries.

However, the written projects and theses of the students reveal that the three different fields or areas are not represented equally in those works. Two thirds of all the written works in Spanish are about culture and society, and, of the last one third, the majority of the works are about literature – according to a count made by Morten Heiberg. This probably reflects a more general pattern and not only the Spanish studies.

We know from the questionnaires that were distributed among the students of Romance languages two years ago, that our students come to us because they want to know about the exotic or powerful and influential foreign places where our languages are spoken, to be able to communicate with people living there. It is evident that they are interested in language, although not as an abstract phenomenon but as a tool that enables them to communicate, i.e. language as a social act, as message and context, yet during their studies they are mostly met with language as a code, a self-sufficient system of inner relationships.

They feel disappointed, as we also know from the questionnaires, and many choose to leave university or to study something else. But why, one may well ask, why are most students of today not interested in the kind of linguistics they meet at the foreign language departments?

One way of answering the question could be by looking at the profile of today's students.

If we look at the demands of young students they can be characterised as follows:

1. The students want the study programmes (and their future work) to be meaningful and challenging.[1]
2. They are very much aware that things change, and that this is a basic condition for themselves as a person as well as for their environments. They perceive the world and their own present situation as temporary or preliminary.
3. The students find limitations in the possibilities of options and alternatives non-democratic and unreasonable. They have been brought up to choose and have experienced that their opinions are important.
4. They are aware that they are responsible for their choices themselves, and that there is very little help available – which means that they are left to their own devices. This also has to do with the status of knowledge. Very few people in our society, if any, have the authority to say what is right and wrong. Identity is not to the same extent as earlier connected to the social background of the person, which also means that students or young people in general often find themselves with difficult choices and few models. Young people of today experiment much more than earlier generations in their need to find their own identity.
5. There is a basic ambivalence in their attitudes – on the one hand a demand for individual choices, on the other hand a demand for the teacher to tell them precisely what they are supposed to know and study.

These facts mean that the students will seek out careers where they find that they can work with something of interest, something exciting, something that challenges and develops them as individuals and helps them to create an identity, something that they find just them! If they feel disappointed they will consequently find it necessary to stop studying – and that is exactly what they do!

---

[1] This is based on a presentation by Lars Ulriksen at the Humanistisk Udviklingsråd's Seminar, November 2000.

Realistically speaking, I think it would be impossible for any syllabus to fulfil all these needs, but the question here is more specifically why studying a foreign language does not fulfill these needs?

My impression is that it is partly due to the concept of language as it is expressed in most teaching of foreign languages today; a concept based on what one could call an anti-subjective tradition of linguistics.

I will elaborate on this hypothesis. Being a historian I have looked for the reason and explanation for this phenomenon in history, i.e. in the processes leading to the present situation. I have chosen to use the works of Foucault to read this history:

In his work 'The Order of Things' ('Les Mots et les Choses'), which bears the subtitle 'An Archaeology of the Human Sciences', Foucault claims that the human sciences, such as psychology, sociology and the analysis of literature and language, are special because they are the sciences where the human person studies him- or herself. The humanities have the human being as both the *Object* of study, and as the *Subject*, i.e. the transcendental basis for understanding and perception. This means that the human sciences can never achieve the same stability as the other sciences; their characters are by definition, and because of this double nature, un-stable.

He also, as we know, traces the history of the human sciences back to the Renaissance in order to explain the historical processes that created the possibility for structuralism to become the answer to the situation within the human sciences at the beginning of the 20th century. He describes how structuralism appeared as a counter discourse within the human sciences to overcome the situation of instability.

Structuralism means a shift from a subject oriented science to an anti-subject science, Foucault claims. If, before structuralism, psychology was interested in the person, the subject telling his or her story, Lacan would claim that the unconscious is structured like language, and that this structure, which it is the purpose of the psychologist to uncover, speaks through the patient. In anthropology we can see a similar development. The focus would be on the structure of the foreign societies, as in the works of Lévi-Strauss. When it came to the field of analysis of texts and language, focus would likewise be on the structure of the text, the structure of language. Whereas language in the Renaissance was one phenomenon among others, in an equal representation of the divine, it gradually changes during classicism and modernity. Structuralism reveals the underlying logic of the system of language, which means that structure, so to say, 'speaks' through language, not the subject or person. Structure is there 'before' the speaking person, it is there whether language is spoken or not.

It seems that Saussure was very well aware of the theoretical and epistemological consequences of the choice he made when he introduced the split between *langue* and *parole*. On the other hand, it also appears as if *langue* during this century has become 'naturalised' to such an extent that these considerations are no longer relevant for the structural linguist when the delimitation of a research project or a course on grammar is planned. If Saussure claims that there must be a 'speaking mass' if there is a language, this fact has long been forgotten and only rediscovered some decades ago in pragmatics and socio-linguistics.

In my opinion, today we are witnessing another shift in the human sciences, a shift away from structuralism, a shift that has been underway for some decades. I think our students express the need for such a shift by leaving the foreign language departments or by not wanting to study foreign languages at all.

They tell us that our concept of language and the study programmes we offer are not in correspondence with their needs and the way they perceive the world we live in. It is very difficult for a person to use the inner logic of a system without a speaking subject as a tool in a process of self-identification. The inner structure and logic of a language system does not help a young person to understand a world of permanent change.

2. Not just modern language studies, but *foreign* language studies

In the title of this conference it says 'Modern Language Studies' and among ourselves at the Faculty we mostly talk about the 'language departments', (as opposed to what we call 'theory departments'!!) But in our departments we do not just study 'language', we study Italian, Spanish, French, Portuguese, German, Dutch etc. All foreign languages! If I want to stress this obvious fact that we are talking about foreign languages it is because it is very often forgotten, and because if we draw attention to it, it has implications.

In the first place it means that we must emphasise the intercultural dimensions of the process involved in learning a foreign language. In the second place it means re-installing the subject, the language user, or the 'speaking mass' in our concept of language. I will explain in detail.

As Gert Sørensen pointed out, there is a need for intercultural understanding today in our societies. This is also due to the fact that the geographical area that we cover is expanding. If the modern language departments could formerly limit themselves to the areas of the European countries where our languages are spoken, this is not so easy today. Voices reach us from distant areas in the languages we thought we knew, and tell us that language can express a counter discourse, a creativity that goes beyond the code of the centre, both challenging and changing it.

For many reasons, some of them mentioned by Gert earlier, we can no longer *not* take these voices from far away and their language into account.

Accordingly, the relationship between language, power, past and present, is challenging us and provoking us to redefine our areas of study.

3. What is intercultural communication about?

There is a whole body of theories addressing this question. In a recent book from the University of Roskilde, Iben Jensen identifies four different research traditions on intercultural communication can be identified. Three approaches have, according to Iben Jensen, often been financed and developed within business or military environments. These are:

1) The literature on 'How to do it', focusing on practical problems facing the traveller or businessmen in their interaction with foreigners.
2) The literature on Intercultural Competence, training and adaptation.
3) The functionalistic research on communications, as for example the 'Reader' by Larry Samovar and Richard E. Porter.

In this book, which has become a classic within the research on intercultural communication, Dorothy L. Pennington argues that:

> The beginning of intercultural communication is cultural understanding – of culture in general, of one's own culture in particular and of another's culture. Before understanding another culture one must fully understand one's own, and therefore a historical background leading to the present state of a culture is necessary. (Pennington, 1972/1991, 31)

In this definition we see a double concern, both for the foreign and for one's own. We can only hope that our students have background knowledge about Danish society, since it is not our primary task to provide them with such knowledge. However, their understanding of Danish culture as *culture* – which is a very different matter – is probably based on experiences with exactly those countries where our foreign languages are spoken. Most of the students have travelled and have knowledge about how Danish culture is perceived from 'the other' – i.e. they already have experiences with intercultural communication, although on a not-conceptualised, non-academic level. These experiences are the ones they want to repeat or qualify when studying a foreign language. They have probably found the intercultural meeting challenging and developing for them as individuals, and their curiosity has been awakened. They have also realised that to communicate fully with the people they have met, they need to speak their language.

A common thing for the first three approaches is the idea of a national culture as the dominating factor in the situation of intercultural communication (Jensen, 2001, 32). This view corresponds with the view of the national languages as being one thing, a system, and a specific and well-defined 'canon', to which all members of the national community have equal access.

Language is, according to Pennington:

> Like culture in general, language is learned and it serves to convey thoughts; in addition it transmits values, beliefs, perceptions, norms, and so on. Through sharing in the language, one becomes a part of a cultural community and has existence in relationship to it. (Pennington, 1972/91, 33)

Although we might agree on the first part of the definition, we also know that things are not that simple any more. We know that many people living in the Danish community have an excellent knowledge of the Danish language, but they are still not accepted as Danes, because their physical appearance is different from the idea of the 'normal' Dane, and because their parents were born somewhere else. This means that being a part of a cultural community and having existence (Pennington, above) is not only a question of self-definition, it has to do with a much broader context – that of society. It means that the individual experiences must be reflected in concepts that also concern social communities and structures, and in the present day context the interface between the local and the global. And it also means that we must realise that there can be many different cultural identities within the same community. This also counts for the societies where our foreign languages are spoken, and consequently it should be taken into account in the concept of language.

The fourth tradition within Intercultural Communiaction studies mentioned by Iben Jensen is the critical, hermeneutic approach. It works with interpersonal communication, and sees culture, as defined by Clifford Geertz, as webs or networks we as human beings spin around us, and tries to work with the definitions that the actors themselves make of their belonging to a specific culture.

This view is interesting in our perspective, since 'definitions that actors themselves make' are expressed in language. It also reminds us of the profile of our students, as young people with a need to construct their identity in a world of uncertainties.

A concept of language that highlights the constructions of identities in a world of changing circumstances can be found, for
example, and I do not think that it is a coincidence, in works about gender and language:

> Language constructs as well as reflects culture. Language thus no longer serves as the transparent vehicle of content or as the simple reflection of reality, but itself participates in how that content and reality are formed, apprehended, expressed, and transformed. (Paula Treichler & Francine Wattman Frank, 1989, 3, cited in Mey, 2001, 307)

Studies on language and gender have long been able to show that language is connected to power. A post-modern approach, however, and especially the works and theories that have been realised within development and post-colonial studies, stress the fact that culture is an arena of struggle. Consequently, if 'language is learned, like culture in general' (Pennington), then language is also an arena of struggle, a way of 'constituting and constructing the world in meaning.' (Fairclough, 1992, 64)

3. Foreign languages and intercultural understanding

We think that the foreign language departments have an important role to play in furthering an intercultural understanding, because of our unique knowledge about the languages, the literature and histories of the countries we are working with.

Each of our fields – language, literature and history/culture – can be seen as important entrances to what could be called the self-understanding of the foreign societies, of how different social agents understand themselves and 'have existence'. The texts we study, in their original language are texts that participate in the constructions of the reality and the ways it is formed, apprehended, expressed, and transformed by the individuals that live in those societies as expressed above by Treichler and Frank.

Although people may not have the same experiences they can still understand each other's meaning (Ashcroft, p. 69), for example, through the fictional universe of experiences. Therefore literature and fiction are unique sources to the self-understanding of the different culture, and also provide unique opportunities for learning about other worldviews, other ways of organising societies and understanding them, which can then make us understand our own world better – and which can function as mirrors in a construction of identity in a difficult world.

This requires however a thorough knowledge of the specific languages, their structures, their histories and the contexts that surround them and that the intercultural aspects of both the language and of the fictional universe are made explicit.[2]

In our view the intercultural aspects call for collaboration between the different fields and traditions within the foreign language departments, literature, history/culture and language.

However, that would require a concept of language where the speaking subject is not the language system, the *langue*, but real, living subjects in a social, cultural and historical context of constant change and creativity, where identity is negotiated and power relations are involved.

---

[2] On the other hand, this should not make us forget the aesthetic dimensions of the fictional text!

We think that such a concept of the foreign language would also be of interest to the student of today, because it would reflect the world they perceive and want to know.

After all – foreign languages give access to the exotic, the challenging and intriguing, the never-ending new world of human beings. Our students have been very wise in their choosing to study a foreign language; it is up to us, as teachers, to show them that they are right.

References

Ashcroft, Bill: 2001. *Post-Colonial Transformation*. London and New York, Routhledge.

Fairclough, Norman: 1992. *Discourse and Social Change*. Cambridge, Polity Press.

Foucaults, M.: 1994. *The Order of Things. An Archeology of the Human Sciences.* New York, Vintage Books.

Jensen, Iben: 2001. *Interkulturel Kommunikation i komplekse samfund.* Roskilde Universitetsforlag.

Mey, Jacob, L.: 2001. *Pragmatics.* An Introduction. Oxford, Blackwell Publishers.

Pennington, Dorthy: 1972. 'Intercultural Communication'. In: Samovar& Porter: 1972/1991.

Raffnsøe, Sverre: 1999. *Historie- eller diskuranalyse? En introduction til Foucaults* Les Mots et les Choses *og* L'archéologie du Savoir. COS Rapport nr. 4/1999, Roskilde Universitet.

Samovar, Larry A. & Porter, Richard E. (ed): 1972/1991. *Intercultural Communication. A Reader* (6th edition). Wadsworth, Belmont, CA.

Ulriksen, Lars: 2000. *Fremmedsprogsfagene set med de studerendes øjne.* Statens Humanistiske Uddannelsesråd.

The Situation of the Foreign Language Studies
"Modern Language Studies in Current Educational Planning"

by

Hanne Leth Andersen

University of Aarhus

The subject of this conference[1] is extremely broad and important, just as Modern Language Studies are. This contribution shall discuss the developments within Modern Language Studies up to now, the present situation, and some perspectives on this.

The key words in this paper are philology, research paradigms and educational goals; thus I offer broad outlines of the issues rather than actual solutions to the current problems. This subject is open for discussion, which is the whole point.

From *traditional* Modern Language Studies to *modern* Modern Language Studies: What is the change that we have experienced over the last century and especially the last decades?

There is quite a leap from the great language and literature professors from the beginning and the middle of the last century, such as Sandfeld, Brøndal, Jespersen, and Togeby, to today's new generation of specialized, comparatively young Ph.D.'s. On the students' side, there is also quite a step from a small group of highly motivated orthodox scholars to the situation of today, in which about 50% of a generation has the qualifications to go to university. And quite logically there is a difference between what it meant and what it now means to study at university.

Politically, decisions have been taken to cut down on the number of years and thus the number of exams that constitute our bachelor and graduate levels.

---

[1] The official language of this conference is English. Some of our colleagues may find this disappointing and not in the spirit of the Modern Language Studies' approach.

The evolution from the great professors is in my opinion also an evolution from philology to science of the humanities, from broad and general knowledge to multi-focused knowledge to specialization. From language and literature in a traditional philological perspective from Antiquity to Modernity, to language and culture in a theoretical perspective, to culture theory, communication theory, media science and intercultural competence – some of the magic words of today.

In fact, one of the most striking things is this opening up of the research field of Modern Language Studies. Within Modern Language Studies it is possible to do research and teaching in what was initially called "civilization" (cf. "civilisation française") but later became society, as well as in politics, gender, media and culture. In the study programmes this last concept can cover everything from tobacco blends to subtitle translation and postcolonial linguistic politics, as is evident from the list of recent Master's theses by students of the humanities at the University of Copenhagen (Danish: 'specialeoversigt').[2] Modern Language Studies seemingly has no limits! Therefore, the option that I am going to defend is specialization within this broad field defined essentially by the specific language studied. In addition, I do not find the notion of Philology quite adequate to comprehend what we do in Modern Language Studies. Actually, it is very difficult indeed to unite our approaches to the common object in one single notion.

Philology could be defined as the study of texts from Antiquity to Modernity; it has a compulsory historical dimension. Texts can, in some definitions, be seen in the broad sense of human products and thereby as interpretations of human nature (cf. Per Aage Brandt 2002; 118). Those of our colleagues who actually call themselves philologists usually establish and edit texts from manuscripts and study those texts. According to Meyers' Fremmedordbog, "Philologi" (I found this reference on the identity debate forum at the Faculty of Arts in Copenhagen[3]) is "den sproglig-historiske Videnskab, der gransker Sproget som et Middel til at trænge ind i et Folks aandelige Liv, særl. dets Litteratur (forsk. fra Lingvistik)". Or, in my translation: "The linguistic-historical science that scrutinizes language as a means to penetrate into a people's spiritual life, especially its literature (different from linguistics)". Again, philology is historical and was connected to the idea of peoples or nations.

The traditional modern philologies were born with romanticism in the 19th century and were very dependent on the concept of nation. One culture, one language – without quite forgetting the oversea areas, the Indians or the other so-called exotic parts of Modern Language Studies. With the

---

[2] Faculty of Arts, Copenhagen: http://www.hum.ku.dk/studieinformation/
[3] http://www.staff.hum.ku.dk/lauha/IDENTITE/identitetsdebatten.htm

introduction of, first, French then, around 1860, English and German to the Danish gymnasium (cf. Hans Bang 1984), Modern Language Studies got a new goal, which was to produce teachers for this educational purpose. And the purpose of Modern Language Studies at the Danish gymnasium was of course culture in the sense of education (Danish: 'dannelse'). The goal was to bring the students to a linguistic level where they would be able to acquire classical French, English or German literature using the model of Classical Language Studies (the study of Latin and Greek). In other words, it aimed towards the perfect understanding of language and texts through grammar and the knowledge these texts offer about culture and society.

So Modern Language Studies got a clear goal for the planning of the study programmes: to study language and grammar thoroughly in order to be able to read and interpret texts. This changes during the 20th century and language studies gets a new goal, that of communication. The evolution within Modern Language Studies touches the concept of culture and language. 'Culture' is no longer the culture of the educated, no longer only learned literature; culture is no longer related to nations.

The situation at present

Today's culture might be intercultural. In the Festschrift for Henning Lehmann (the retiring vice-chancellor of the University of Aarhus), Per Aage Brandt (2002) discusses different conceptions of education ('dannelse'):

(1) "[…] individuals who do not share "history" in any substantial respect, and who do not share language, still communicate. They are able to learn, to acquire each others' styles. Therein rests their "education". This point is decisive: "education" overcomes as a principle historical-cultural closedness." (Brandt 2002; 120, my translation)

(2) "If a culture is such a normative filter, […] then education, the way I see it, lies in overcoming this filter's shaping of communication and cognition, an overcoming that is possible by virtue of the acquisition of something bigger, that is the perspective of knowledge ("erkendelse")." (Brandt 2002; 123, my translation)

Being educated could have to do with cultural openness, with intercultural skills, as in the first definition where the ability to communicate is a modern definition of education, which is what Per Aage Brandt – not without critics – seems to suggest in the first quotation. In the second, the notion of education is somewhat larger; it is not just being able to communicate in spite of different cultures, but arriving at a higher level of knowledge. I guess one of the main themes of today is just this. What are the humanistic and academic norms of today's society? Those norms are the ones we valorise and choose to study; those norms determine our research areas and our educational strategies. Not because politicians want this, but simply because we are part of society.

Scholars of the humanities used to study literature and language; culture was literature and art. This is no longer sufficient; we talk about a more complex world, information society, mass media, mass culture and internationalisation. Our key concepts are still culture and language, but they cannot be isolated, as culture is no longer only so-called good literature and good language; culture is endless and so is language, and the historical dimension is not compulsory any more, though it is part of our understanding of the present and constitutes an important context for our studies. Philology is no longer the proper word; Language and culture studies seem more appropriate.

The new dominating scientific paradigm in the twentieth century was structuralism, or describing language and texts as structures. We still struggle with this intelligent and abstract vision, as Anne Marie Jeppesen shows in her paper (this volume), but many things have happened since the sixties. The linguistic dimension is no longer limited to the study of phonology, morphology and syntax, but also encompasses pragmatics, sociolinguistics, psycholinguistics, ethno-methodological discourse analysis, conversation analysis and intercultural communication analysis. In linguistics, the object is no longer only an abstraction, *langue*, and the goal is no longer only to establish the system, but also to study its manifestations and the relation of those manifestations to situation, medium, genre, culture, identity, acquisition and communication. The concept of language has indeed changed. But it does take time. Teachers who studied modern languages quite a few decades ago carry out much of the language teaching at secondary school. At university, grammar tends to be supplemented by disciplines that present the new ways of understanding language. At the French Department in Aarhus, we present first-year students with a subject called "Language and Communication", where we introduce them to language in general, the structure of our study programme with special reference to areas where language and language skills play a role, and the modern linguistic paradigms: pragmatics, argumentation theory, variational linguistics, and language acquisition.

I think there has been quite a parallel evolution in literary studies: the focus is no longer on the establishment of the structures that characterize texts, the explanatory procedures, but very much on understanding. The interpretational process is explicitly double and combines structures with an understanding that goes beyond the text. If I'm not mistaken, this would be the vision of Paul Ricœur.

It is clear that we are well on our way to moving beyond structuralism on the basis of strong concepts defined by structuralism. But this does not solve the multi-focus problem. The three or four dimensions of Modern Language Studies cover most of what you can possibly study, and on top of that they are all endowed with a possible but not compulsory historical or diachronic dimension. This is probably a very natural state in an information society. But it confuses our students, it does not appeal to our politicians, and it is criticized, with some justice, by scholars such as Hans Hauge, senior lecturer at the English Department of the University of Aarhus (for example, in the Danish Newspaper *Information*, 4th of September 2001), who likes to say that you can study almost anything within Modern Language Studies, and that nobody is interested in the results because they are isolated, unconnected, and unmotivated.

Now the big question is whether Modern Language Studies should constitute 'mini-universities', as some have called this new form. Should our object be everything that is connected to the language we study, everything that is connected with the area in which this language is spoken? No wonder our students sometimes get confused and ask themselves what the point is. You can see this by consulting, for example, the very interesting Student Survey at the Romance Department of the University of Copenhagen.[4] And no wonder our politicians ask us to define the core disciplines and competencies (Danish: 'kernefaglighed')?

Luckily, professors and scholars of Modern Language Studies have not disappeared from the public debate, but have formulated new propositions as to what the point is. In *Uddannelsesredegørelsen* (2000), Peter Harder asks for what he calls paradigmatic examples of the specific goal of each branch of the humanities; these are precise, practical examples rather than formal, theoretical ones; for instance, in the study of English, he suggests one core competency for our students to aim at: being able to give an account of a text like King Lear that brings together in a competent way linguistic features, knowledge about feudality, the world order during the specific period and the sharp confrontation between values that Shakespeare sets up.

This would also be my vision as regards the strength of Modern Language Studies. The important thing is to define broad core competencies that combine our fields of studies instead of creating a hierarchy where we distinguish core and periphery. Peter Harder explicitly warns against the using the metaphor of core in opposition to periphery. The question is whether as modern specialized researchers we can incarnate this model and pass this ideal on to our students. The problem they sometimes point out is that each of us works in our own field, we each have our own theory, and we expect the broad synthesis of knowledge to take place in the students' heads. This seems even clearer at some faculties of arts than at others.

---

[4] http://staff.hum.ku.dk/hp/Spoergeskema/Spsm1_32.htm.

Actually, faculty politicians have tried to organize faculties in new ways, sometimes separating research and studies to a certain extent. This is the case at the University of Southern Denmark in Odense. Linguists are in one department, literature and culture researchers in another, historians in yet another. The study programmes and the students belong to centres: Centre for Spanish, Centre for English, and so forth. This model has chosen the standpoint that modern researchers in German linguistics have little in common with researchers in German literature, or at least they have more in common with researchers in Spanish linguistics or in general linguistics. Students still study all three dimensions, and the educational planners have to think of them jointly. But bringing them together as in Peter Harder's example may not become more evident in this way.

At the University of Copenhagen and the University of Aarhus, the organisation of the Faculties of Arts is the object of many interesting discussions. Their choice at the moment seems to be not to split up modern language researchers, whether they work in the field of linguistics, literature, culture or social science. The specific language still determines the common interest. We defend this with reference to the specific approach that Modern Language Studies offers.

I think that if we want our students to see a point in studying all of these different domains, then we ourselves must be engaged in some kind of common project. I am not convinced that this project is what Hans Lauge Hansen calls Culture Philology, because it defines our research in a very specific, yet broad, manner. It could make specialization more difficult, and specialization is part of our identity as researchers at present.

When it comes to study programmes, we must define the core disciplines together, we must find the points that we share: the sociologist and the linguist might share discourse analysis, pragmatic theory and sociolinguistics; the literary theorist and the linguist might share narrative theory, for example. The approach to the object is what you may call 'modular', but the object is the same, and only by a combination of the various theories can we come to a somewhat complete understanding of it. This is the force of language studies compared to the purely theoretical approaches: a broader knowledge of the object's connection to the culture from which it stems, a deeper knowledge of its language.

I believe that our research is actually strong because of this deeper perspective we have on texts and their contexts, because we specialize on the background of broad knowledge about a certain linguistic area. This is what makes our research different from that of a general linguist, a scholar in literary theory or a sociologist. The project is ambitious, and with new theories appearing we do have some difficulty in defining the core competencies (in a non-hierarchical definition) and especially the limits of Modern Language Studies. And it is true that the researchers that incarnate the project, the comparatively young Ph.D.'s who are employed at Modern Language Departments, are becoming more and more specialized. Students also want to specialize, and they want to know why we teach grammar, old English, 16th century literature, elections in France, deconstructivism, mass media and so forth.

I think the answer lies in that same specialization. General basic knowledge in several scientific disciplines and, at a higher level, specialization, the possibility to choose your own profile among a certain number of modules. The force in this being the focus on method and a general knowledge about the object. Linguistic knowledge and language skills can also be differentiated, as Karen Sonne Jacobsen (2001) suggests. Not every student needs the same morpho-syntactic level of correction; some might focus on pragmatics and communication. This gives our students the possibility of focusing on what interests them and seeing the point of studying languages. Let them combine specific interests with good knowledge of a foreign language in its cultural context. We must hold on to this, we must not give up serious language and culture studies based on original texts for translations and global English as our lingua franca, which might be the alternative: to study theory and texts in English or in Danish translations and to take a language course to learn to communicate in more exotic languages such as Spanish, Italian or German.

Our society, our industry, our private and public sector – in short, *we* do not want a monolinguistic society. This could in its turn lead to unidimensionality and a lack of cultural consciousness, a lack of education in both of the senses described by Per Aage Brandt. And this is where we talk about a crisis today. Foreign languages do not appeal to young people as much as they did 30 years ago. Very few students choose other languages than English their last year of high school. Three out of four students in the modern language section in Danish high schools choose English. Only one out of seven in the same section, the language section, choose French during their last year of high school.[5] In addition to this, the concept of language teaching and language learning at the Danish gymnasium is more and more focused on language, the literary dimension becoming more and more difficult to reach with fewer lessons available and just two years of language studies at the normal C-level. There are experimental classes proposing "European literature", just as at the Faculty of Arts in Aarhus we are going to propose courses on "World literature". Such very interesting courses risk separating language and text, the literature being often studied in English or Danish translations, which is so much more practical – just as we find it more practical to speak English here today.

---

[5] Cf. Danish Industry publication about the Danish gymnasium: "Gymnasiet i forandring. Fremtidens almene gymnasium".

But we do need a real understanding of languages in order to understand texts and culture, in order to call ourselves educated. Knowledge of languages constitutes a necessary prerequisite for acquiring the cultural insight capable of again making real communication and intercultural understanding possible. One of the main ideas expressed by Hans Lauge Hansen is that the language studies must be capable of conveying a conscious and theoretically reflective way of creating a link between the language, the culture and its imaginary world picture and selfknowledge as mirrored in art and literature. The conscious and reflective way of creating this link between language and culture as mirrored in art and literature could be what we ask of our students with Peter Harder's King Lear example. But as a specific theory in itself, this global approach is not necessarily one that all modern language theorists can agree with. The way we believe we can fulfil the task is by studying language and culture from different points of view, in a modular understanding, maybe not in a strictly conscious modular way, but by trying to describe and explain our object from many points of view; each theory, each result being conceived as a module. We can conceive that together these different modules may give us a somewhat true and complete picture.

The more global, semiotic project of culture philology wants to attack the object at its very centre. This is tempting, and an enormous task, though not impossible, but it cannot and does not unite linguists, literary theorists and sociologists. The complexity of the object makes us run the risk of creating too abstract, too theoretical an approach.

I think that modern linguists are more and more conscious of the cultural, social, pragmatic, psychological, and cognitive contexts of language. Literary studies are also increasingly open to cultural contexts, and culture studies are of course at the very centre of this project. So we do approach the object in ways that focus on the link between language and culture, only the way I would prefer to conceive our common points is by thinking in different, specialized modules.

What are the new perspectives of Modern Language Studies on educational planning and educational politics?
Politicians, Danish industry, the private and public sectors, and the Danish system of secondary education do not only have a need for common general knowledge, but also specialization and flexibility.

Since our departments are not exactly growing – we have witnessed over the past five or six years a spectacular reduction in the staffs of the Modern Language Departments – the new tendency goes towards an opening up of the faculties, towards letting our students also study history at the History Department and specialize in information studies or media at the Department of Information and Media Studies. I believe that if we want to maintain Modern Language Studies as educational unities – and the need to know languages and cultures well is obvious – then we must allow a certain opening up of the faculties of arts. And thus give our students the opportunity to specialize in a conscious way. The foundation, the first two years of the Bachelor degree programme, must not only provide a general introduction, but also show some of the more tasteful parts of the studies, the core competencies rather than just the core disciplines, which are sometimes inherited from another period's vision of language studies. At the graduate level, then, it should be possible to specialize.

Once again, one of the practical problems is language! If we work together with literary theorists, linguists and sociologists, which language should we choose to speak and in which language should we read the texts? I would suggest the reading of original texts in the main European languages and discussions sometimes in groups in other languages than just Danish and English, and I think this kind of problem should not be an obstacle to this collaboration. Sometimes the theoretical problems are not as relevant in practice.

It has been mentioned that we should distinguish between different specialized branches in our study programmes; thus we might offer, for example, grammar and language acquisition studies for future language teachers, more socially related programs for candidates who want to work in the private or public sector, and rhetoric and presentational skills for future information workers.

There are several good reasons for avoiding this separation inside Modern Language Studies. First of all, it is expensive. Grouping students in several smaller pre-established branches costs more than having them attend the same lectures. Second, flexibility is needed. Students must be able to combine, for example, modules from linguistics – such as argumentation theory – with modules from sociology in order to create a profile that puts emphasis on their personal profile and strong points. Third, we are not sure, for instance, that the best future secondary school teachers are those who know a lot about grammar. Knowledge about general psycholinguistics, linguistic norms and language acquisition is a good thing for future teachers, but so is broad cultural knowledge or perhaps specialization in film, theatre or modern poetry.

Lars Ulriksen from the University of Roskilde has pointed out that today's students seek studies that are meaningful to themselves as individuals and to their own personal development.[6] Lilli Zeuner (2000) emphasizes that young people today want to construct their own education, and this is what

---

[6] In his contribution to a conference organized by Danish 'Humanistisk Uddannelsesråd': "De videregående sproguddannelser – er der behov for reformer?" (2000).

especially Modern Language Studies must take seriously, because of the extreme and inevitable broadness of the study object.

Conclusion: So how should we see ourselves? Do we still have a common identity?
Our common identity lies in the specific language, whether this be spoken in one country or in several parts of the world. Our object is this language in its cultural and social context. Such an object must be approached and studied from many angles, within many theories, isolated or combined in order to give us, our students and the society we live in a profound knowledge about it. This knowledge is essential not only to us, but to our society and our culture.

Therefore, we must be able to motivate our students to study modern languages. And I think that in this respect we should focus on elements that convey the new theoretical approaches and that are required in our students' future job functions. Some of these elements could be the following: communication, culture, intercultural communication, discourse analysis, argumentation, rhetoric, oral and written presentation skills. We must formulate the core competencies towards which we aspire, not only core disciplines, which risk creating hierarchies instead of a global understanding of our object. And we must not force our students to be multi-focused, but rather to do as we do: specialize while keeping our eyes wide open to other approaches to the common object – language and culture.

References
Bang, Hans: 1984. "Fransk på gymnasialt niveau 1809-1984", *Fransk og dannelsen.* Fransklærerforeningen, pp. 30-50.
Brandt, Per Aage: 2002."Humanistiske meditationer", *Dannelse, Uddannelse, Universiteter.* Festskrift til Henning Lehmann den 31. januar 2001, pp. 118-127.
Harder, Peter: 2000. "Nogle betragtninger om begrebet 'kernefaglighed'", *Uddannelsesredegørelsen,* pp. 133-137.
Sonne Jacobsen, Karen: 2001. "De andre sprog – om sprogvalg og sproguddannelser", *Sprogforum 19,* pp. 22-28.
Zeuner, Lilli: 2000. *Unge mellem egne mål og fællesskab. Værdier og valg blandt elever i de studieforberedende ungdomsuddannelser.* Socialforskningsinstituttet.

The Cultural Turn of Philology

by

Herbert Grabes

University of Giessen

Let me start by quoting a few sentences with which the British sociologist David Chaney begins his recent study *The Cultural Turn*:

> In the second half of the 20th century the theme of culture has dominated the human sciences. Concepts of culture have generated perspectives and methodologies that have challenged orthodoxies and attracted the energetic enthusiasm of young scholars. More significantly, the forms of contemporary culture demand a radical reappraisal of the terms of description of the modern world. We therefore need to consider our options when culture does not just provide the meaning of experience but is also the terms of that experience. (Chaney 1994; i)

And there is indeed no question that 'culture' has become the central concept for those academic disciplines traditionally termed the Humanities or *Geisteswissenschaften*. Under the sway of postmodern epistomological scepticism, the search for what holds true for all humanity seemed futile and was replaced by an investigation into the relative validity of the cultural constructs held to be true only within certain regions of the world at a particular time. Thus 'culture' as a regionally and temporally limited sphere of consensus regarding those constructions of meaning that determine the experience, knowledge and description of the world and the self has come to serve as the last horizon of reference for a postmodern anti-metaphysical way of thinking. And as the 'Geist' of the *Geisteswissenschaften,* both in its humanist-individualist conception and its collectivist meaning either as 'Volksgeist' or the metaphysical Hegelean 'Weltgeist', could also no longer serve as an integrating concept within the compass of that sceptical stance, the various disciplines belonging to that sphere of the academy have resorted to 'culture' as a new centre of their common endeavour or rather a new horizon within which their traditional borderlines can be overcome in view of new interdisciplinary projects and goals. The humanities have become 'Kulturwissenschaften' (cf. Anderegg/Kunz

1999), disciplines engaged in the investigation of various aspects of culture.

When thus all the disciplines within the humanities have turned to culture, there seems to be nothing special in the cultural turn of philology. Yet I hold that we are dealing here with a special case, and before I come to the new chances this turn opened up for philology, I will first try to show why philology in its traditional sense of the historical study of language and literature has been threatened by the general turn to culture. In order to do this, I have to say a few words about how this turn has come about and what it implies. As to the question of origin, one has to see that culturalism, the recent view that almost anything is cultural, is based on a conception of culture as a social construction, the sphere of all collective human endeavour to understand and confer value on experience – both the experience of the world and the self – by signifying practices, and that this concept is a result of the fact that twentieth-century philosophy has been dominated by the philosophy of language. Beginning with Wittgenstein and Saussure and continued by structuralism, analytic philosophy, deconstruction and poststructuralism, the explication of our experience of the world and the self has been determined by the model of language (cf. Grabes 1992; 1-20). The human being has been understood as a signifying animal, constructing cultures as collective identities of various kinds by signification. The constructed character of 'culture' becomes most clearly evident in almost all recent histories of the concept, from Roy Wagner's *The Invention of Culture* (1981) to Chris Jenks' *Culture* (1993), David Chaney's *The Cultural Turn* (1994), Adam Kuper's *Culture: The Anthropologist's Account* (1999), Thomas Jung's *Geschichte der modernen Kulturtheorie* (1999), Terry Eagleton's *The Idea of Culture* (2000), Francis Mulhern's *Culture/Metaculture* (2000) and Friedrich Kittler's *Kulturgeschichte der Kulturwissenschaft* (2000).

Particularly influential, however, for the dissemination of the semiotic view of culture has been more recent American ethnology. As is well known, culture was treated by Clifford Geertz in his study *The Interpretation of Cultures* (1973) as webs of signification, where cultural practices appear as signifying practices. And because under this assumption a particular culture appears as a complex text that has to be interpreted in much the same way as a difficult literary text, it is literary criticism and scholarship with their strategies of interpretation that seem to possess the best methods for cultural research. It is therefore no wonder that scholars in English Departments suddenly felt particularly qualified to engage in cultural studies and cultural history at large and left their traditional field of investigation.

A similarly powerful move towards the conception of culture as a text that can and has to be 'read' and interpreted came from semiotic theory as developed by Thomas E. Sebeok, Umberto Eco, Walter A. Koch and Ronald Posner. And regarding cultural history, an additional most powerful influence has come from Foucault with his metaphorical use of 'discourse' in his interpretation of culture as a power-driven 'discursive formation'. We find this influence as well in the New Historicists' endeavour to relate actual texts to social performances and events (cf. Veser 1989; Greenblatt/Gunn 1992) as in British Cultural Materialism (cf. Colebrook 1998; 175-197), and the various contributions to Tamsin Spargo's recent critical anthology *Reading the Past* give further evidence of such an approach.

We also have to see that this conceptualization of culture on the basis of the model of language went along all too well with postmodern constructivism and anti-foundationalism as theoretical underpinnings of the liberation movements of feminists and gays as well as with the foundationalist identity politics of ethnic minorities. What we are dealing with is not any longer culture in the general anthropological sense of universal forms of life, but particular cultures as webs of signifying practices constructing group identities of various kinds and sizes. Dealing with the history of particular languages and literatures, traditional philology therefore seemed to be on the right track, but it came to be looked at as being much too narrow in its scope under the assumption that culture as a whole was created by signification and that the whole of cultural history had to be read as the history of signifying practices. Thus philology looked outdated because the model of language was too successful. When under the perspective of deconstruction culture as a whole was to be seen as a text ("...il n'y a pas de hors-texte...", as Derrida put it)[1], and semiotics held that culture could best be described as a system of signs, the philologist as a specialist in textual interpretation had to become a reader and interpreter of culture. Even if one didn't go as far as stating that culture *was* a text, one could at least say that all communication within culture and about culture, all cultural knowledge, all evaluative processes and all making of distinctions within culture took the form of special kinds of discourse (for instance political, legal, economical, historical and so on). Especially the socially most important distinctions of class, race and gender thus have come to be analysed as results of cultural 'writing' in a host of publications. And when one realizes that under this assumption human individuals also appeared as being 'written' by the culture into which they had been born and to which they had been assimilated by education – even to the point of the unconscious being structured like a language, according to Lacan –, one can see why it looked very attractive to those who had been

---

[1] Derrida 1976; 158.

trained as philologists to start reading all kinds of cultural phenomena including the human subject as texts.

Especially those who had been dealing with literary texts in the narrower sense, that is, texts for which a particular status of literary works of art had been claimed, now recognized that within this new paradigm of culture not only those, but all kinds of texts or discourses had become important. A good example is the New Historicists who started to attribute to non-literary texts a degree of attention formerly reserved only for literary texts. Indeed, the privileging of a particular corpus of texts as 'literature' was no longer seen as something given but treated itself as a cultural construct. Especially in the US this led to veritable 'culture wars' about the opening of the canon (cf. Atlas 1990; Jay 1997) within which feminists claimed the traditional neglect of women authors (cf. Fendler 1997) and the spokesmen of cultural minorities the exclusion of texts not belonging to traditional Western culture. Philologists who continued to focus their work on the traditional canon were accused of supporting a kind of academic institution that was suppressive in conserving patriarchal and Eurocentric values. Thus Barbara Herrnstein Smith as president of the Modern Language Association in her presidential forum of 1988 advocated a "radical destabilization of the domain of literary studies" and had no qualms in risking that this discipline might be "effectively and undeniably undone" (Fleischman 1995; 813).

Yet there was another threat to traditional philology that came from those who retained the more traditional notion that culture in terms of the 'cultural sphere' was only a part of the overall makeup of society. Not least due to the increasing impact of the new media, mass communication and popular entertainment they started to investigate the advent, institutionalization and function of the various technologies of representation such as print, lithography, photography, film, television and the internet as well as the older and more recent forms of popular culture. In Britain Stuart Hall and his colleagues at the Birmingham Film Institute (cf. Hall 1980; Turner 1990; Agger 1992) linked their new endeavours to the older work of Richard Hoggart, Raymond Williams and Edward Thompson, who had investigated British working class culture in a remedial way against the predominance of what was then termed elitist or high culture and thus did much to establish a new kind and field of investigation. This looked very attractive to young scholars in English Departments who saw new research opportunities that absolved them from writing another article on Milton or Wordsworth or T.S. Eliot and also gave them the feeling that their work was more relevant within the context of present mass culture. With the years even relatively conservative publishers like Oxford University Press devoted quite a few pages to "Media and Cultural Studies" within their "Literature" catalogue, advertising books with topics like *British Youth Television*; *The Feminist, the Housewife, and the Soap Opera*; *Dumb-Struck – a Cultural History of Ventriloquism*; *Black Hunger: Food and the Politics of US Identity*; or *Sinophiles and Sinophobes: Western Views on China*.

What one also finds in this and other catalogues devoted to "Literature", is a particular section on "Theory". The cultural turn I have tried to describe has not only been instigated but also accompanied by an impressive output of theoretical studies extending from *Theories of the Text* and *Psychoanalysis and the Scene of Reading* to *The Melancholy of Race: Psychoanalysis, Assimilation and Hidden Grief*, and *What is a Woman?* or *Nietzsche's Ethics and his War on Morality* – to quote just a few titles from the same catalogue.

*

After my provisional genealogy of the cultural turn and a scanty description of the impact of this turn on the recent development of philology I would now like to focus on the future role of philology within the *Kulturwissenschaften* and the new research opportunities opened up by the focus on culture. What has first to be pointed out is that within the new overarching paradigm of *Kulturwissenschaften* the various academic disciplines within the humanities have to operate on the assumption that their field of enquiry - be it the political or social structure of society, education, religion, history, art, language or literature - has to be seen as only one among many aspects of a common culture, aspects with a very limited autonomy so that their multiple links with other cultural fields must not be neglected. They have to become and remain self-reflexively aware of the fact that their findings may be valid only for a limited phase of a particular culture, that their methodology is largely determined by the current conventions of the academy, and that their very existence is not naturally given. This means that each academic discipline has to keep in mind its position and its special function within the presently valid construct of academic pursuit and finally within the whole structure of present culture. And this means that we are all much more in need of theoretical self-reflection than we have ever been in the past.

As to the academic discipline of philology, its traditional task has been the description and analysis of language and literature in their historical development and cultural embedding. Within the Eurocentric organization of academic disciplines it has, however, not been institutionalized as a general discipline (as is the case for instance with sociology or history). Instead, the language aspect of culture is investigated within separate disciplines, each dealing with the domain of one particular language or at best a family of closely related languages, that is in the English or German departments, the departments of Romance, Scandinavian, Slavic or Arabic languages and so on. This means that every philological discipline also deals with the culture or cultures whose language and literature it is devoted to – not least because the function of language and literature can only be determined within the cultural context; yet it is language that determines the field of investigation of the particular philological disciplines.

And it has to be stated that this continues to make sense within the new paradigm of the humanities as *Kulturwissenschaften*; for there can only be an interdisciplinary investigation of a particular culture if the various disciplines involved are able to contribute a detailed knowledge of the various domains and aspects of culture as a whole. Especially in view of the central role attributed to language within culture the various philological disciplines with their close study of particular languages and literatures as well as their function within particular cultures will be able to make valuable contributions.

Yet philology has undoubtedly taken the cultural turn, and probably its most striking impact has been the extension of the field of investigation under the heading 'Cultural Studies'. On the assumption that culture is a 'text' in terms of a complex construct of signification, there is no feature or aspect of culture that cannot become the object of investigation in philology as a discipline specialized on the interpretation of texts. And if one looks at the range of topics dealt with in Cultural Studies one can indeed come to the conclusion that a kind of super-philology has begun to take over the work of sociology, history, psychology and philosophy. Yet if thus the range of possible objects of investigation has become almost unlimited, it seems the more necessary to clearly limit the perspective under which the various features and aspects of culture are approached by philology. What seems to me most important is that the philological approach to culture will be clearly defined as a semiotic one, both in terms of a concentration on the various modes and codes of signification that are essential for the construction of cultural identity and in terms of a focus on the recurrent valuations established and supported through these codes, valuations making up those culture-specific hierarchies of value that determine the way of thinking, feeling and acting within a given culture (cf. Belsey 2000; Grabes 2001). On a more abstract level we can say that what philology now is dealing with is recurrency within the whole domain of textual signification: recurrency in terms of the patterns and structure of language as investigated by hard-core linguists; recurrency in terms of genres, subgenres, strategies of presentation, aesthetic form, the history and migration of motifs and themes as studied by literary scholars and critics; and now for some time also recurrency in terms of textual manifestations of cultural practices and culture-specific valuations as examined by Cultural Studies. This links philology with anthropology, which has always focussed on recurrent behaviour in terms of ritual; it also links philology with sociology, which depends on the recurrency of social behaviour and social positions for all its findings; and it also links philology with psychology, especially Lacanian psychology because Lacan holds that the unconscious is structured like a language and defines individual identity as insistent behaviour (Lacan 1977). If philology investigates in which way particular ways of thinking, feeling and acting are preferred, tolerated or rejected in and through language, it can make a specific and very important contribution to the study of culture within the context of the various disciplines that see themselves as *Kulturwissenschaften*.

This has various consequences for the further development of philology. Besides being devoted to literature as literary art, philology will have to deal with and feel responsible for the professional analysis of all kinds of language discourses and discursive formations, and it will have to give particular attention to the way in which the manner of representation contributes to the establishment and dissemination of a particular system of evaluation within a given culture. In other words: philology will be responsible for the analysis not only of the forms of language discourse, but also of their particular function for the establishment and safeguarding of the hierarchy of values that largely determines or even makes up a culture as a whole. This also implies that philology – as it has already begun to do – will have to study the specificity and cultural role of the various means or media of representation, that is it will be responsible for the analysis not only of written texts appearing on paper or in the new digital media, but also of the semiotics of the auditory and visual media such as radio, television, film and the internet. In doing so it will, of course, have to co-operate with the new disciplines specializing on the new media and to make use of the findings of the psychology of auditory and visual sensation and perception, but as the aspect of language and signification plays an important role within these media, it is one consequence of the cultural turn that philology will also have to deal with this aspect of culture (cf. Wenzel 1999). And we just have to think of the ubiquity of story-telling and of the kind of presentation we know from drama to see that philology can add an important perspective to the analysis of a feature of our present culture that has developed into a veritable culture industry.

Due to its expertise regarding signification, philology has also a large stake within the new cultural history with its preference for representations, signifying practices, discursive formations or networks of symbolization as objects of enquiry. Owing to the widely shared conception of culture as a text, the activity of the cultural historian is seen as a kind of reading, a present ascription of signifieds to the traces of the past that are taken as signifiers (cf. Spargo 2000; Grabes 2001). For the greatest part these traces are anyway language texts of various kinds, but also regarding paintings, maps, monuments and architecture philology can help to find the best guesses at past significations by applying the Saussurean model of language, that is, by focussing on the recurrent patterns of collocations, combinations and oppositions and thus ascertaining the once dominant relations between signifiers that determined their meaning. In addition to that, philology can then also help to discover the network of symbolic values that made up a culture of the past – disseminated valuations in terms of idealizations, preferences, rejections or indifferences which align into hierarchies, a network Roland Barthes has called "myth" in order to point out that it makes what is cultural look natural to those who live in and by it (Barthes 1957). And if the result of such an enquiry should be that there are several competing hierarchies of value to be found within one and the same society at a given time, philology may also give some proof for the assumption of the new cultural history that the traditional constructions of homological, 'authentic' past cultures are mere illusions of an older historiography looking for organic wholes.

New research opportunities due to the cultural turn have also been opened up for philology by an increased attention to what I would like to call the cultural history of literature as a particular strain of cultural history at large. In systems theory of the Luhmann kind, this domain of enquiry has been designated as the 'literary system' (cf. Schmidt 1989). Yet even without subscribing to this theoretical frame, one can speak of a cultural sub-system made up of the conditions under which authors have written, the way literary texts were disseminated, the kinds of readership authors addressed and who the actual readers most probably were, and the promotion of certain texts and conventions of writing by critics and literary historians who wrote about them and included them in a literary canon. In the last few years I have been involved in a project dealing with the creation of the canon of 'English literature' through the writing of literary histories, and it is interesting to see how the writing of histories of English literature in Britain, for instance, has been placed within written culture at large and has formed at various times a central pillar in the building of a national tradition, of a treasury of innovative and otherwise outstanding writing from the past that served to prove the excellence of national culture. In this way the work of philology becomes also closely linked with the new investigations into the creation of national identity as an imaginary construct as they have been promoted by Anderson, Hobsbawm/Ranger and others. The cultural history of 'literature' also deals with the essential question of what kinds of texts have within a given culture at various times been included in a particular canon of 'literature' in a narrower sense and thus been granted a special prestige. Bourdieu has spoken in this regard of a "field of restricted production", a field in which legitimation and symbolic value are conferred by "consecretation", a "consecretation performed by writers, critics and literary historians who – together with editors and publishers taking care of the dissemination and preservation of individual works – have decided about their public value" (Bourdieu 1985). The history of literary criticism and the history of the writing of literary history are thus of primary importance for the cultural history of literature.

Yet however much the cultural history of literature can demonstrate the influence of culture at large and its various institutions on the creation and preservation of a corpus of texts valued as 'literature' or 'poetry', and however much our understanding of the literature of the past depends on our being acquainted with cultural history, I would finally also like to point out that literary works in terms of professed fictions may just as well demonstrate the limits of the culture from which they arise as mirror its dominant preferences and ideas. For in being a history of a 'fictive institution' (Derrida 1992; 36), that is, in creating a space for what culture otherwise excludes or marginalizes, the history of the functions of literature is also a history of culture's Other, of the historically changing limits of culture and of the awareness of those limits made evident in attempts to at least imaginatively transgress them. One further important research opportunity opened up by the cultural turn of philology is therefore a new history of the functions of literature that deals with the relationship between the artificial world-making in literary texts, that is, in texts with a "suspended relation to meaning and reference" (Derrida 1992; 48), and that one in the discourses in which this relation is not suspended. This particular kind of history can reveal to us to what extent the freer space of literary discourse has been used to either lend an imaginary validity to hierarchies of value propagated by the hegemonic powers and/or collectively desired, thus disseminating and sustaining the current ideology; how literary discourse has been used to make visible the gap between such idealizations and the actual conditions and way of life to foster a critical stance; and how far, by presenting marginalized, repressed or merely excluded world-views and values it enabled its readers to become aware of the alternatives to the prescribed, desired and lived values prevailing. One of the effects of recent culturalism, particularly in the wake of Foucault, has been the dissemination of the view that it is almost impossible to escape the limitations of a given culture (a view shared by New Historicists with traditional Marxist critics who see art and literature primarily as a manifestation of ideology). Yet it is worth noting that Marxists like Althusser and Macherey have pointed out that the literary work of art by achieving through its formal composition an "internal distancing" from the ideology from which it arises will "make us perceive" that ideology (Althusser 1971; 204), that by "mingling the real uses of language in an endless confrontation", by "experimenting with language rather than inventing it, the literary work is both the analogy of a knowledge and a caricature of customary ideology", and is therefore able to reveal ideological illusion as constructed (Macherey 1966; 59).

If thus the neglect of form is extremely detrimental to cultural history (cf. Thomas 2001), it has to be said that literature can just as easily exceed the limits of the prevailing culture or expose conflicts within that culture through *what* it presents, that is by using the free imaginary space to promote values thematically in exemplary stories, stories ranging in their mode from overt allegory to strictest realism and wilful fancy.

What remains to be added is a reminder that such a history of the functions of literature must not be restricted to a linking of literary texts to the cultural past within which they were produced. As is especially the case with canonical literary texts, and for English literature the works of Shakespeare would be a prime example, by being preserved, disseminated, widely read or performed at later times and different stages of culture, they also acquired different cultural functions. The same values exhibited in a work that were once transgressive or indicative of an emergent culture may well have come to appear to a later readership or audience as being representative for the then prevailing or a merely residual culture, or the other way around. This is so because the signifiers of the past lend themselves not only to an attribution of those meanings informed by a knowledge of the culture within which they were produced. Their interpretation is also subject to the inclinations and needs of those living in the later culture within which they are newly approached. The functional history of literature will therefore also have to integrate the history of reception as – at least in part – a history of culturally induced 'misreading'. And we can make plausible guesses about what the particular function was only if we compare the choices faced and inherent evaluations attempted with those that appear to be dominant in other discourses of the time. If literature cannot be reduced to being a manifestation of the ideology current at the time of its production, it can also not be expected that it will always have been or even remained subversive. It might just as well exemplify valuations and evaluative hierarchies that were commonly desired or even demanded yet imperfectly realised or direly wanting in the culture within which it originates or to which it has come down. Hence the actual function of an individual literary text or a whole genre in a given culture remains the subject of historical enquiry. Literature may use the imaginary space to tighten or to loosen the grip of a dominant culture, either by helping a residual one to persist a little longer or by stimulating an emergent one to come into its own a little earlier. With literature, it is difficult to calculate the effect; and this is why literature will remain suspect to all planners and controllers. Precisely for this reason, for its potential to transgress the limits of past cultures but also of our own culture, the endeavour to reinvigorate the collective memory of literary works of the past and to promote attention to the literary works of the present have been and will be the most important contribution of philology to our present culture, for it will help us to see better the limits of this our present culture and thus enable us to redraw those limits in the future – redraw them in view of a hopefully more enlightened vision of human beings and society.

References

Agger, Ben: 1992. *Cultural Studies as Critical Theory*. London, Falmer.

Althusser, Louis: 1971. "A Letter on Art in Reply to André Daspre". *Lenin and Philosophy and Other Essays*, transl. Brewster, Ben: 1966. London, New Left Books.

Anderegg, Johannes and Kunz, Edith Anna, Hg.: 1999. *Kulturwissenschaften: Positionen und Perspektiven*. Bielefeld, Aisthesis.

Anderson, Benedict: 1983. *Imagined Communities*. London, Verso.

Atlas, James: 1990. *Battle of the Books. The Curriculum Debate in America*. New York, Norton.

Barthes, Roland: 1957. *Mythologies*. Paris, Editions du Seuil.

Belsey, Catherine: 2000. "Reading Cultural History". Spargo, Tamsin, ed., *Reading the Past*. Basingstoke, Palgrave, pp. 103-17.

Bourdieu, Pierre: 1985. "The Market of Symbolic Goods". *Poetics* 14, pp. 13-44.

Chaney, David: 1994. *The Cultural Turn: Scene-setting Essays on Contemporary Cultural History*. London and New York, Routledge.

Colebrook, Claire: 1998. *New Literary Histories. New Historicism and Contemporary Criticism*. Manchester and New York.

Derrida, Jacques. "'This Strange Institution Called Literature': An Interview with Jacques Derrida". Derrida, Jacques: 1992. *Acts of Literature*, ed. Attridge, Derek. London and New York, Routledge, pp. 33-75.

Derrida, Jacques: 1976. *Of Grammatology*. Transl. Gayatri Chakravorty Spivak. Baltimore, The Johns Hopkins University Press.

Eagleton, Terry: 2000. *The Idea of Culture*. Oxford, Blackwell.

Eco, Umberto: 1968. *La struttura assente*. Milano, Bompiani.

Eco, Umberto: 1973. "Social Life as a Sign-System". D. Robey, ed., *Structuralism*. Oxford, Clarendon Press.

Fendler, Susanne, ed.: 1997. *Feminist Contributions to the Literary Canon: Setting Standards of Taste*. Lewiston, NY, Lampeter, Edwin Mellen Press.

Fleischman, Avrom: 1995. "The Condition of English: Taking Stock in a Time of Cultural Wars". *College English* 57, pp. 807-21.

Foucault, Michel: 1966. *Les mots et les choses*. Paris, Gallimard.

Foucault, Michel: 1969. *L'archéologie du savoir*. Paris, Gallimard.

Geertz, Clifford: 1973. *The Interpretation of Cultures*. New York, Basic Books.

Grabes, Herbert: 1992. "Die Welt als Text. Postmoderne Texttheorie und Weltbild". *Wissenschaft und neues Weltbild*, Vorlesungen, Giessen, pp. 1-20.

Grabes, Herbert: 2001. "Literary History and Cultural History: Relations and Difference". Grabes, Herbert, ed., *Literary History/Cultural History: Force-Fields and Tensions*. Tübingen, Narr, pp. 1-34.

Greenblatt, Stephen and Gunn, Giles, eds.: 1992. *Redrawing the Boundaries. The Transformation of English and American Literary Studies*. New York, Modern Language Association of America.

Hall, Stuart: 1980. "Cultural Studies: Two Paradigms". *Media, Culture and Society* 2. No. 1, pp. 57-72.

Hobsbawm, Eric and Ranger, Terence, eds.: 1980. *The Invention of Tradition*. Cambridge, Cambridge University Press.

Hoggart, Richard: 1957. *The Uses of Literacy*. London, Chatto and Windus.

Jay, Gregory S.: 1997. *American Literature and the Culture Wars*. Ithaca, NY, Cornell University Press.

Jenks, Chris: 1993. *Culture*. London and New York, Routledge.

Jung, Thomas: 1999. *Geschichte der modernen Kulturtheorie*. Darmstadt, Wissenschaftliche Buchgesellschaft.

Kittler, Friedrich: 2000. *Kulturgeschichte der Kulturwissenschaft*. Munich, Wilhelm Fink.

Koch, Walter A.: 1986. *Evolutionäre Kultursemiotik*. Bochum, Brockmeyer.

Kuper, Adam: 1999. *Culture: The Anthropologist's Account*. Cambridge, MA, Harvard UP.

Lacan, Jacques: 1977. *Ecrits: A Selection*. London, Tavistock.

Macherey, Pierre: 1966. *A Theory of Literary Production*. Transl. Wall, Geoffrey: 1978. London, Routledge.

Mulhern, Francis: 2000. *Culture/Metaculture*. London and New York, Routledge.

Posner, Ronald, Hg.: 1997. *Semiotik. Ein Handbuch zu den zeichentheoretischen Grundlagen von Natur und Kultur*. Bd. 1. Berlin and New York, de Gruyter.

Sales Catalogue "Literature 2000-2001": 2001. Oxford, Oxford UP.

Schmidt, Siegfried J.: 1989. *Die Selbstorganisation des Sozialsystems Literatur im 18. Jahrhundert*. Frankfurt/M., Suhrkamp.

Sebeok, Thomas E.: 1975. *The Tell-Tale Sign – A Survey of Semiotics*. Lisse, De Ridder.

Sebeok, Thomas E.: 1994. *An Introduction to Semiotics*. London, Pinter.

Spargo, Tamsin, ed.: 2000. *Reading the Past*. Basingstoke, Palgrave.

Thomas, Brook. "Figuring the Relation Between Literary and Cultural Histories". Grabes, Herbert, ed., *Literary History/Cultural History: Force-Fields and Tensions*. Tübingen, Narr, pp. 341-358.

Thompson, Edward: 1963. *The Making of the English Working Class*. London, Victor Gollancz.

Turner, Graeme: 1990. *British Cultural Studies*. London, Unwin Hyman.

Veser, Aram, ed.: 1989. *The New Historicism*. New York, Routledge.

Wagner, Roy: 1981. *The Invention of Culture*. Chicago, University of Chicago Press.

Wenzel, Horst: 1999. "Kulturwissenschaft als Medienwissenschaft". Anderegg und Kunz, *Kulturwissenschaften: Positionen und Perspektiven*. Bielefeld, Aisthesis, pp. 135-154.

Williams, Raymond: 1958. *Culture and Society 1780-1950*. London, Chatto and Windus.

Williams, Raymond: 1961. *The Long Revolution*. London, Chatto and Windus.

A Change of Paradigm in Language Studies[1]

by

Hans Lauge Hansen

University of Copenhagen

A New Philology of Culture
Given the precondition that the traditional *Geisteswissenschaften* have changed into *Kulturwissenschaften,* as stated by, among others, Bernd Henningsen (Henningsen 1997, 14), a new philology of culture would have to define itself as being concerned with the relation between languages and cultures. In his 1996 article "Litteraturwissenschaft, Kulturwissenschaft, Anglistik" Herbert Grabes saw the actual importance of Cultural Studies within the Humanities as a result of the influence of postmodernist deconstruction and different constructivist positions. According to Herbert Grabes, the constructivist approach to cultural studies represents an opportunity to restore the unity of the Humanities as such, and of Philology in particular. The romantic concept of the national spirit, the *Volksgeist,* that gave unity to the philological enterprise in the nineteenth century, might be exchanged with the concept of culture in the twenty-first century, perhaps enabling us to re-establish the lost unity of the philological quest.

This seems to be a very promising perspective: the theoretical compartmentalisation of philology may be overcome by an interdisciplinary effort to scrutinize the relationship between language and culture, between literature and culture, between history and culture and so forth. But is it one and the same thing we are talking about when we use the word "culture" in these different combinations, and does it make any sense to talk about culture as one homogeneous and undivided entity?

---

[1] This paper is the expression of my own personal opinion, and it cannot be ascribed to the foreign language commission of the University of Copenhagen. One part of this article is going to be published under the title "Towards a Philology of culture" in Hans Julio Jensen (ed) *The Object of Study of the Humanities* (forthcoming).

This is evidently not the place to start a discussion about the concept of "culture", but it is important to say that "culture", understood as a closed and homogeneous whole, an independent island surrounded by water, must be replaced by more open, dynamical and constructivist approaches (Wilken 2001, Hastrup 1999, Altmeyer 1997). A new philology must conceive of culture as an open, multi-voiced and dialogical interaction full of contradictions, and less as a deterministic, homogeneous and closed structure. Culture could be analysed according to Norbert Elias' "Prozes-soziologische Zivilisationstheorie" as proposed by Claus Altmeyer, or it could be seen in the light of Lotman's description of the *semiosphere*, as proposed by Stephan Michael Schröder, i.e. as the *locus* of a creative interaction, where human communication is understood as translation processes across cultural borders (Schröder 1997, 92). Anyway, this change of theoretical focus implies that the object of study becomes fragmented and multifaceted, and this is why the cultural dimension within foreign language studies must consist in building up intercultural and hermeneutical competences in the individual student rather than conveying a certain amount of knowledge (Altmeyer, 1997; 9).

Another question is whether there ever existed an academic unity within traditional philology that we can aim to *re*-establish. National philology emerged as the result of the positivist and the hermeneutical trends of the nineteenth century, but did these trends really merge into a unified academic enterprise at that time? In *The Order of Things* Michel Foucault mentions "philology" as one of three empirical sciences, decisive for the creation of the modern episteme at the end of the seventeenth century. But with the term "philology" Foucault exclusively refers to the discipline of linguistics. According to Foucault, philology or linguistics were founded as an empirical science based upon a comparative methodology and under inspiration of the natural sciences. Friedrich Schlegel expressed it in this way as early as in 1808:

> Jener entscheidende Punkt, aber, der hier alles aufhellen wird, ist die innre Structur der Sprachen oder die vergleichende Grammatik, welche uns ganz neue Aufschlusse über die Genealogie der Sprachen auf ähnliche Weise geben wird, wie die vergleichende Anatomie über die Naturgeschichte Licht verbreitet hat. (Schlegel, *Über die Sprache und Weisheit der Indier*,1808, p. 28)

Linguistics established itself as a "positive" science that intended to dissect language as the anatomists dissected the human body, by focussing on the linguistic system and leaving the representational function of linguistic discourse out of sight. In Foucault's wording:

> This displacement of the word, this backward jump, as it were, away from its representative functions, was certainly one of the important events of Western culture towards the end of the eighteenth century. (Foucault, English ed. p. 281)

Literary criticism, on the other hand, was mainly based on a hermeneutical tradition, and was characterized by Foucault as: "the contestation of philology (of which it is nevertheless the twin figure): it leads language back from grammar to the naked power of speech" (Foucault, English ed. p. 300). So, according to Foucault, linguistics and literary criticism, positivism and hermeneutics, never did merge within traditional philology, and I think that he is right on that point. From the beginning, linguistics conceived of itself as a heritage from the natural sciences, and based itself on a positivist methodology.

It is, however, much more doubtful whether linguistics can maintain this immaculate position today, although it managed to survive Foucault's epistemological revision. Is it not the case that the pure positivist position, extrapolated by linguistics from the very birth of national philology and maintained during the twentieth century, is itself an inseparable part of the ideological construction of the nation states? Is it not the case that this ideological commitment only becomes visible now, because the present state of the art within the humanities requires a more conscious methodological meta-reflection of each of the disciplines involved? Herbert Grabes writes that:

> [D]er Konstruktcharakter jeder Einzeldisziplin von ihr immer mitbedacht werden muß, wenn sie nicht in einen naiven Ontologismus zurückfallen will – dass heißt: Sie ist in viel stärkerem Maße theoriebedürftig im Sinne der Selbstreflexion ihrer Stellung und Aufgabe innerhalb des kulturspezifisch geltenden Wissenschaftkonzepts und letzlich der jeweiligen Gesamtkultur. (Grabes 1996; 377)

It is through this kind of metareflection within the specialized disciplines that the epistemological questions hidden at the root of their creation suddenly surface, and a series of new questions arises: How did the sub-disciplines of traditional philology conceive of their object of study? How did the positivist and the hermeneutical methods relate to each other within these sub-disciplines, how did they develop during the twentieth century, and how do they relate to each other today? If my hypothesis is true, traditional philology insisted on a pure positivist approach for ideological reasons. In order to explain this I would prefer to go on to the epithet of the "new" in the title.

The concept of the "new"
In my proposal for a philology of culture I have stressed the word "new", not only because I want to define it in opposition to the "old" philology, but as a reference to the "new philology" within medieval studies. In his introduction to the 1990 issue of *Speculum,* Stephen Nichols presents what might be called a programme for the "new" philology in opposition to traditional or national philology. In his article entitled "Philology in a manuscript culture", Nichols states that traditional philology conceived of

the medieval text as a singular, linguistic entity, whereby the manuscript's original complexity and diversity was reduced. By applying a methodology inherited from classical philology, traditional nineteenth century philology manipulated the medieval texts as part of an ideological agenda concerning the construction of the nation state and an "imagined community" in the form of a distinct national culture. In contrast to this approach, the "new" philology of medieval studies sets out to explore the texts in their materiality as many-layered potentials of multi-voiced signification: the palimpsest character of the different hands of different scribes, the commentaries in the margins or interpolated in the texts, the visual images and other iconic devises and so forth. Nichols states that: "the *new* philology ... reminds us that ... we need to embrace the consequences of that diversity, not simply to live with it, but to situate it squarely within our methodology" (Nichols 1990; 9).

In this introduction Nichols shows that it is equally impossible to eliminate either the meticulous positivist elaboration of the philological detail or the hermeneutical interpretation within the philological quest. Therefore the new philology establishes itself as a search for a mediated relationship between positivism and hermeneutics; it is able to do so because it liberates its object of study from what Grabes called naïve ontologism, and it does so as a result of the methodological self-reflection mentioned above.

It is my hypothesis that the concept of "dialogue" could be seen as an adequate metaphor for a series of parallel epistemological changes within the Humanities, of which the "new philology" of medieval studies is only one. The dialogue has been used as a metaphor for human reflection since Plato; it has been characteristic of the description of the general semiosic processes in Charles Peirce; it has been used by Bachtin to describe the basic linguistic principles of human communication, and it has been used as an image for the hermeneutical understanding by Schleiermacher and Gadamer etc. etc. These philosophers, and probably many more, may all be understood as part of the common precondition for the emergence of a paradigm of dialogised thinking, but the proper epistemological change concerns more precisely the recognition of the dialogical principle in the construction of the very object of study, a process that has taken place within the last 15 years. In the following, I will go on with the explanation of the ways in which this change affects our understanding of key philological concepts such as "text" and "language".

The concept of the "text"

The concept of the "text" has been discussed by Paul Ricœur on several occasions, and I think that the development in his philosophy might be taken as representative for the emergence of a new dialogised relation.

In 1970 Ricœur wrote an article entitled "What is a text?", in which he argued in favour of a theory of textual interpretation that integrated positivist explanation and hermeneutic understanding as two distinct and yet interdependent approaches. He took his point of departure in a critique of Wilhelm Dilthey, to whom the concept of "explanation" belonged to the natural sciences, while the concept of "understanding" belonged to the humanities as a proper and adequate category of hermeneutic interpretation. As an alternative to Dilthey's absolute separation of the two approaches, Ricœur stated that both the natural sciences and the humanities were in need of both positivist explanation and hermeneutic understanding, and, under the influence of the dominating structuralist theoretical paradigm of the day, Ricœur described "explanation" within the field of textual analysis as the analysis of textual structures in order to reveal the semantic deep structure of the text, while "understanding" was seen as the individual reader's hermeneutic appropriation of the text in Gadamer's terms.

As a result, what Dilthey wanted to conceive of as an ontological difference between the object of study within the natural sciences and the humanities respectively, now in Ricœur's thought of the seventies became separate approaches to the same object, but with different methodological skills and goals (ie. structuralist explanation vs. hermeneutic interpretation). In his book *Time and Narrative* from the mid-eighties, however, Ricœur distinguished between the text as a reservoir of possible significations and the act of reading as an actualisation of one part of this possibility. This meant that the relation between the signification of the text in itself and the interpretation of it in the act of reading, which was first described as two distinct methodological processes, only a few years later was construed by Ricœur himself as two inseparable modal aspects of one and the same process of interpretation.

The new position represents a cognitive and pragmatic turn, through which a dialogised relation between the positivistic and hermeneutic processes becomes possible. In the case of textual interpretation, this implies that our only access to the text, understood as a reservoir of potential significations, lies in the actual reading of it, which *per se* is inseparable from hermeneutic interpretation. Where Ricœur's former position presupposed that the signification of the text existed in itself and, so to speak, before the actual reading, the dialogised position posits that the text, understood as a potential of signification, only exists as a critical parameter of empirical control within the reader's construction of the hermeneutic meaning in the act of reading.

A dialogic concept of textual meaning therefore implies that the signification of the text is not something inherent or immanent within the linguistic structure of the text, but something emerging in the process of reading. The empirical reader consequently must be regarded as the main source of the produced meaning, leaving the text in the role of the critical parameter of empirical control. This may seem absurd considering that we normally hold that "this book says so and so" etc. But then again, it is obvious that a book cannot make a reader understand what he or she is not prepared for. In this sense, a book is a tool for thinking and it is the empirical reader's responsibility to do what Umberto Eco calls his "philological home-work" in order to be able to produce a meaning equivalent to the meaning the ideal "model-reader" would produce (Eco 1981; 91). The appropriateness of the concept of the model-reader has been criticised by, among others, Richard Rorty, in whose opinion there is no difference in terms of correctness or legitimateness between one reading and another, even if one is erudite and scholarly and the other totally individual and fortuitous (Eco 1995; 102). But if we follow Umberto Eco's line of thought, any text, including the literary one, could be regarded as an index or as a series of indices that the reader has got to trace and fill out in order to recontextualise the text culturally and unfold its semantic richness. The purpose of the discipline of literary studies within the foreign language departments would consequently be to prepare the students in this sense, i.e. provide them with the knowledge and analytical competencies required for the cultural and intertextual recontextualisation of the text in the act of reading.

However, different formalist approaches to literary studies have prevailed during the second part of the 20th century in the majority of the departments of literature throughout the western world, and I do not think that the literary studies within the foreign language studies are any exception in this regard. New Criticism, Russian and Czech Formalism, different Structuralist and Semiological approaches etc. all have one thing in common, and that is the belief in the autonomy of the text. And as pointed out by, among others, Wlad Godzich, this is exactly the reason for their success (Godzic 1998; 26). Notwithstanding their theoretical differences, they are all very apt to deal with a situation in which an increasing number of students enter the universities in order to engage with academic studies, as it has been the case in all the Western countries since World War II. The increasing amount of new students necessarily implies that a growing number of individuals enter the universities without the cultural background that in former times could be taken for granted. This is why an approach to the study of literature that focuses exclusively on the textual fragment at hand and the rhetorical close-reading of it, seems very appropriate to this situation, and provides at least one explanation of the reason why literary studies have had theoretical formalisation on their agenda to such a degree throughout the 20st century. In his 1958 introduction to his *Literatursprache und Publikum in der lateinischen Spätantike und im Mittelalter*, Eric Auerbach states that cultural competence required by the reader in order to make the kind of historically and culturally contextualised interpretation that has been characteristic of his own work, cannot be taught as a kind of methodology (Auerbach 1958). It is the result of many, many years of reading and a rare kind of individual sensibility, and not something that can be taught or included in a syllabus.

Although it is always difficult to generalise, I think that the approach to literary studies within foreign language studies in Denmark has more or less followed the same pattern as described above. Given the poor preparation of the students and the limited time at hand for the introduction to the vast field of literary studies within our departments, we have to a certain degree focused on the presentation of a series of analytical procedures and formal models (narrative schemes, actantial structures, rhetorical concepts etc). This has inevitably happened at the expense of the intertextual and contextual relations necessary for the interpretation of the text as a cultural phenomenon. And I think that I myself, with my contributions within the field of textbook-editing must bear part of the responsibility for this on my shoulders (Hansen 1993 and 1995).

This being said, it must be added that formalisation and theoretisation are necessary. Conceptualisation and theoretical reflection are necessary in order to convey the kind of metareflection mentioned above, and we cannot afford to lose three thirds or more of a generation of students anyway. So, what has to be done about it? I think that the solution must be found in the formalisation or application of the pragmatic, reader-oriented and cultural approaches that will allow us to establish a series of interdisciplinary relations needed in order to make the students themselves take advantage of one discipline within the realm of the others. As for myself, I have started this work within literary studies with some short presentations of a functionalist approach to literature, drawing upon a Lotmanian concept of the literary text understood as a model designed for the interpretation of culture and society (Hansen 2001b and Hansen, forthcoming 2). In this work I attempt to bring pragmatically oriented semiotic models (Charles Peirce and Michail Bachtin) to bear on readings of literary texts, with the intention of schematising the reader's testing and evaluation of ethical and moral values and subsequent creation or construction of different aspects of his or her cultural identity through the identification with and/or rejection of imaginary experiences of the fictitious subjects.

The concept of "language"
Under the influence of structuralist thinking, language has been understood as a monolithic structure that anticipates and determines both culture itself and all that it is possible to say, write or even think within this culture. Today, however, this concept of language has been deconstructed, and the former "naturalised" concept of language appears to be an ideological construction that emerged on the precondition that a national culture had to have one language. As Lisanne Wilken puts it, "different languages exist because they are singled out, classified, given name and cultivated as such in the processes of political power that have taken and

still take place in Europe" (Wilken 2001; 179). This implies that the stipulated scientific positivism of traditional linguistics was always related to an ideological enterprise. And Suzanne Fleischman posed the same question when she stated that linguistics in the beginning of the twentieth century had to constitute an object of study that was stable and homogenous in order to separate itself from the historical and textual activities of philology: "the scientificity of linguistics ... is founded on an illusory object: a stable, unitary, monolithic entity that has no existence in linguistic reality, but rather, is a construct of linguistic practices, an object of our own fabrication" (Fleischman 2001; 44).

The ideological glass splinter of national philology has been stuck in the eye of the ice-queen of linguistics right from the very start. And you might therefore ask if the deconstruction of the naturalised or ontologised concepts of "language", "nation" and "culture" has not obliged linguistics to break back into the study of living discourse and merge with hermeneutics?

Foucault operates with three major epistemological changes in the history of Western thought since the fifteenth century: the Renaissance, the Enlightenment and Modernity. One of the major differences between the Enlightenment and Modernity consists in the degree of confidence that scientific investigation has in linguistic discourse. The Enlightenment saw science as an encyclopaedic project of ordering the world through linguistic discourse. Modernity, however, lost faith in discourse and focused on the systems and structures governing our conscious life behind our backs, for instance in biology, economy and linguistics. Within linguistics, what happens is that the overall focus of interest becomes the comparison of the linguistic systems between different languages. Foucault says:

> The threshold between Classicism and modernity ... had been definitively crossed when words ceased to intersect with representations and to provide a spontaneous grid for the knowledge of things ... Once detached from representation, language has existed, right up to our own day, only in a dispersed way: for philologists, words are like so many objects formed and deposited by history; for those who wish to achieve a formalization, language must strip itself of its concrete content and leave nothing visible but those forms of discourse that are universally valid. (Foucault 1966, English ed., p. 304)

In this quotation Foucault states that language within linguistics "right up to our own day", that is 1965, has been studied as an abstract system cut loose from actual representation, i.e. linguistics has not been dedicated to the study of the living discourse. But what has happened since then? I think that recent theoretical trends and interdisciplinary approaches to the study of the relationship between languages and cultures, some of them presented here at this conference, have made linguistics return to the study of the living discourse. But of course, it is not each and every pragmatic approach that allows for a real and genuine integration of linguistics and cultural studies. Today many linguists are dedicated to the description of different particles of language and their function within the system of language syntactically, semantically and pragmatically, but that is not what I mean by breaking back into the study of living discourse. As a rough guideline Antje Hornscheidt's discrimination between two forms of pragmatics will suffice: an additive form and an act oriented form (Hornscheidt 1997, 194). The additive form is supposed to be a kind of pragmatic theory in which pragmatic aspects of language are added to the genuinely unpragmatic understanding of language as a systematic structure, whereas the act oriented form of pragmatics is directly based on the language use. While the first form, according to Hornscheidt, gathers different kinds of Psycho-, Neuro- and Sociolinguistics, the second form is represented by Critical Discourse analysis and Explicative Semantics.

A change of epistemological paradigm?
Yesterday at this conference it was mentioned in the debate, that a simple exchange of words within a dialogue between two people would not appear to be linguistically interesting, unless it could be explained as part of how the system of language works. With all due respect for the linguists within the audience and submitting myself to the risk of being accused of chasing ghosts, I would say that this attitude could be seen as a perfect example of the modernist paradigm of science at work. According to the modernist paradigm, the interest governing scientific investigation is directed towards the structures that rule everything behind our backs, and the answer to the scientific quest is expected to reveal the systems of relations beyond the reach of the human subject's immediate cognition (the accumulation of capital, the unconscious of the human psyche, the system of *langue*, etc.). Therefore Jostein Børtness in his paper accused modernism of being authoritarian, and thererfore Anne Marie Jeppesen in her contribution to this volume has called for the reintroduction of the human subject within the linguistic practice, and I think that both commentaries are of some relevance here. Referring myself to the same example I would say yes, it would be interesting what a guy says to his girlfriend, if we could possibly say something about the way in which he declares his love and how this way of doing things belongs to a cultural practice. I acknowledge that this requires a certain amount of formalisation and systematisation in order to describe the system of practices that characterise a certain culture, and therefore I am not speaking against the abstraction of analytical concepts. What I am speaking for is another distribution of interest between recurrence and variation in class-room teaching, in order to use Herbert Grabes' concepts. If recurrence represents the recurring habits that give stability to cultural practices, linguistic as well as non-linguistic ones, and coin them as such, then each and every discourse is also an instance of variation in as much as it is a single and unique event. And I think that it

is this event-character of linguistic discourse that interests the majority of our students, and I think that it is the competencies related to the analysis of language as discourse or social practice, that may provide the foreign language studies with an immense social relevance within the era of globalisation.

We all agree that language is not a transparent tool. It makes a difference in what language a text is written or read, and in the foreign language departments we insist upon the importance of reading the original texts in the original languages. We even make this issue one of the main differences between for instance the foreign language departments and the departments of comparative literature, where they read the texts from outside the traditional western canon in translation. Languages are asymmetrical, says Lotman, and therefore each and every translation has got to be considered the creation of a new text (Lotman 1990a). In this process the very linguistic form becomes loaded with meaning, and suddenly the comprehension of the meaning of form, or aesthetics, appears to be something inevitable in the study of the relation of linguistic discourse to cultural practice.

The fact that the relation between languages and cultures even today remains a question that is heavily loaded with ideology, becomes depressingly clear when you listen to the actual xenophobic debate about migration and the problems related to the integration of the minorities in Denmark. But according to Lisanne Wilken, even the European Union builds upon such ideological prejudices generated by national romanticism, and linguists are used for ideological purposes every day, because the description and the recognition of a language as a such gives the right to claim cultural independence in some way (Wilken, 181). And this is nothing new. The number of national languages increased at a faster rate between 1800 and 1900 under the influence of national romanticism than in any of the preceding ten centuries, and between 1900 and 1937 the number of Europe's standard languages increased more than in the thousand years before (Wilken, 177). National ideology sees "language" as equivalent to "culture", and not as a means with which, or through which, cultural identities are construed. And national ideology presupposes national identity to be more important, more "deeply rooted", or superior to other kinds or cultural identity like gender, class, profession, political orientation etc.

Although these questions are not new, nor untreated within academic disciplines, the foreign language departments as such are not, at the moment, in a position to present a theoretically reflected point of view on how the relation between linguistic discourse and cultural identity are to be understood and analysed in general. Individual scholars, and even small scientific communities within our departments that work with issues related to this topic, might be able to formulate answers to this question. But as institutions we are not prepared to give an answer, and until we are,

I am afraid that it will be the romantic notions of language and culture as naturalised and interrelated entities that will prevail among the majority of students and even among some teachers, until we are able explicitly to present an alternative.

If the foreign language studies want to develop a studies programme and a line of investigation, giving priority to the relation between languages and cultures, we must confront this ideological dead weight from within all of our disciplines. One might say that this is not an adequate subject for linguistics or literary studies, but then again I would like to remind you of the definition of traditional philology, that may be found in almost any dictionary or encyclopaedia from the late 19th or early 20th century. Here is the 1924 definition of the concept of philology from the Spanish Espasa-Calpe encyclopaedia:

> Philology is the science that has as its object a people's or a group of people's spiritual character as it is reflected in the ancient or modern language and literature. In this way, language in general is not the object of the philological inquiry, nor is literature in general, but only and exclusively the language and the literature of a specific people.
>
> ...
>
> Philology only and exclusively becomes a science by using the investigation of linguistic and literary studies that characterize it, as a tool or an instrument for getting to know the character or spirit of this or that people or group of peoples. (*Encyclopedia Universal Ilustrada*, Espasa-Calpe 1924. My translation)

If we leave out the romantic notions of national spirit etc., we still have the question of how languages relate to cultures as the approach that unites the different disciplines within philology, and I think that this would be a very useful and productive perspective for all the disciplines within the traditional philological departments to engage with. In order to promote an increased interaction and interdisciplinary collaboration between the, as it were, balkanised disciplines of the foreign language departments, we should begin to change our disciplines from within, trying to relate each and every discipline to the global perspective of a philology of culture. I am fully aware that changes do happen all the time within each of the different disciplines, but mostly on an individual and local basis. And I am afraid that the specialisation of the disciplines has already gone too far to hope for the capability of the individual teacher to be able to cope with the whole field covered by the foreign language studies. I therefore believe that the time has come to start a discussion across disciplines in order to cultivate all the different possible approaches to the study of the relations between languages and cultures. Elsewhere I have posed three main questions, as one set of possibilities among others, which might help us to point out the field of investigation opened up by interdisciplinary approaches. The questions were (Hansen 2001,II): 1) What is the function of language in the construction of social relations and cultural identity? 2)

What is the function of literature in the construction of cultural identities? And finally 3) What is the function of language in the construction of the imaginary universes of literature? Following these three questions I proposed a series of theoretical approaches that might help us establish important relations between the three main disciplines of the foreign language studies. Among other things I stressed the possibility of making historical and social sciences relate to linguistics by analysing linguistic discourses and speech acts as social practices. I argued for the importance of the interpretation of narrative structures and rhetorics to historical studies, I stressed how pragmatics and reception aesthetics are turning literary studies towards the study of the construction and experimentation with cultural experiences and identities, and I pointed to the general importance of the pragmatic turn of linguistics towards language as a living discourse. When this is said it should be added, however, that this project is not a question of having everybody doing everything, but a question of collaboration between professionals. We should not force anybody to do anything, really, because this would only create resistance and lead to pure amateurism. The individual freedom of choice in regard to theoretical framework and scientific methodology in both teaching and investigation should not only be respected, but even cherished as a way to avoid monological and closed solutions.

And then again, the overall orientation of foreign language studies towards the investigation and explanation of the many different sets of relations between languages and cultures should be reinforced and cultivated. We must recognise that within many areas of investigation a change has already taken place, and we should dedicate ourselves to the, in my opinion, most rewarding study of how we might turn this into a general change of profile of foreign language studies. A change within the syllabuses and class-room practices of the different language studies, that matched the emergent change within at least part of the ongoing investigation, would not only meet the demands and interests of contemporary students as described by Anne Marie Jeppesen, it would also be a way to respond to the overall change of epistemological paradigm that reorients the human sciences towards the living discourse. The interest of the human sciences is no longer exclusively oriented towards the anti-subjective and authoritatively closed systems, ruling our actions and ideas behind our backs like for instance economy, psychodynamics or grammar. The human sciences of the 21st century will have to engage themselves in the study of the human agency within the cultural processes. And this requires a return to what I have been calling the study of living discourse. Not to the authoritative and monological discourse that, according to Foucault, characterized the encyclopaedic project of enlightened despotism and that delivered the rational grid for the monological representation of truth, but rather to an open, dialogised and unfinalized discourse of unlimited semiosis, through which we not only represent the world, but also construe our own presence within the world. The centre of interest for a new Philology of Culture must be the multivoiced and dialogised discourses, that characterise the production and distribution of knowledge in the globalised information society.

If language as a living and dynamic discourse is always situated within a historical context, it will no longer be necessary to divide the human sciences between the historical and formal approaches to their object. That our object of study is a construct means that we should focus on the linguistic character of the cultural and historical issues, but at the same time we must consider the historical character of language itself. Likewise, a dialogised relation between positivist and hermeneutic approaches should make us focus on the historical character of the formal object; but at the same time we must formalize the understanding of the historical processes. The dialogised position makes it possible to mediate between positivist and hermeneutic approaches, and thereby overcome some of the limitations inherent in either of the two.

The dialogical change of the epistemological paradigm represents the possibility for a re-actualisation of the philological enterprise. It is not an option to restore the unity of the disciplines of traditional philology, because such a unity hardly ever existed; instead we must create a new and genuine platform for the development of a broad variety of interdisciplinary approaches to the relation between languages and cultures.

References

Altmayer, Claus: 1997. "Zum Kulturbegriff des Faches Deutsch als Fremdsprache". *Zeitschrift für Interkulturellen Fremdsprachenunterricht*, 2, 2.

Auerbach, Eric: 1958. "Om hensigt og metode", *K&K* 92, 2001.

Bassnett, Susan: 1998. "The Translation Turn in Cultural Studies", Bassnett & Lefevere (eds): *Constructing Cultures*. Clevedon, Multilingual Matters.

Brøgger, Frederik Chr: 1992. *Culture, Language, Text: Cultural Studies within the Study of English as a Foreign Language*. Oslo, Scandinavian University Press.

Corbet, Noel: 1992. "What's New in Philology?" *Romance Philology* 46,1.

Eco, Umberto: *Fortolkning og overfortolkning*. Gylling, Systime.

Eco, Umberto: 1981. *Lector en fábula*. Barcelona, Lumen.

Encyclopedia Universal Ilustrada, 1924. Madrid, Espasa-Calpe.

Fleischman, Suzanne: 2000. "Methodologies and Ideologies in Historical Linguistics: On Working with Older Languages". In: Herring, Reenen & Schøsler: *Textual Parameters in Older Languages*. Amsterdam, Benjamins.

Foucault, Michel: 1966. *Les Mots et les Choses*. Galimard. English edition: *The Order of Things*, New York, Vintage Books, 1994.

Godzich, Wlad: 1998. *Teoría literaria y crítica de la cultura*. Frónesis, Cátedra, Madrid.

Grabes, Herbert: 1996. "Litteraturwissenschaft, Kulturwissenschaft, Anglistik". *Anglia* 114, 3.

Hansen, Hans Lauge: (Forthcoming 1). "Towards a New Philology of Culture". In: Hans Julio Jensen (ed) *The Object of Study of the Humanities*. Copenhagen.

Hansen, Hans Lauge: (Forthcoming 2). "Erfaringsbearbejdning som dialogisk proces i litteratur". In Jan Lundquist & Nina Møller Andersen (eds): *Smuthuller*. Bachtinselskabet i Danmark.

Hansen, Hans Lauge: 2001. *For en ny kulturfilologi I & II*. Web article available on http://www.staff.hum.ku.dk/lauha/IDENTITE/Debatforum/

Hansen, Hans Lauge: 2001b. "Semiotik". In: Fibiger et al (eds): *Litteraturens tilgange*. Copenhagen, Gads Forlag.

Hansen, Hans Lauge: 1993 and 1995. *Tegn, tekst og tolkning*, First and Second Editions. Copenhagen, Akademisk Forlag.

Hastrup, Kirsten: 1999. *Viljen til Viden*. Copenhagen, Gyldendal.

Henningsen, Bernd: 1997. "Das Ende des Humboldt-Kosmos". In: Henningsen & Schröder (eds.), *Vom Ende der Humboldt-Kosmen*. Baden-Baden, Nomos Verlagsgesellschaft.

Hornscheidt, Antje: 1997. "Der *Linguistic Turn* aus de Sicht der Linguistik", In: Henningsen & Schröder (eds.), *Vom Ende der Humboldt-Kosmen*. Baden-Baden, Nomos Verlagsgesellschaft.

Lotman, Yuri: 1990a. *Universe of the Mind*. Bloominton, Indiana University Press.

Lotman, Yuri: 1990b."Über die Semiosfäre", *Zeitschrift für Semiotik*, 12, 4.

Nichols, Stephen: 1990, "Philology in a manuscript culture", *Speculum* 65, 1.

Nielsen, Henrik Kaare: 2001. *Kritisk teori og samtidsanalyse*. Aarhus University Press.

Richardson, Peter: 1994. "The Consolation of Philology", *Modern Philology*, 92,1.

Ricœur, Paul: 1970. "What is a text?" In: *Hermeneutics and the Human Sciences*. Cambridge University Press, 1981.

Ricœur, Paul: 1983-1985. *Temps et Récit*. Editions du Seuil. English edition: *Time and Narrative*. University of Chicago, 1984-1988.

Schlegel, Friedrich: 1808. *Über die Sprache und Weisheit der Indier*. Heidelberg.

Schröder, Stephan Michael: 1997. "150 Jahre Begriffstradition von Kulturwissenschaft". Henningsen & Schröder (eds) *Vom Ende der Humboldt-Kosmen*. Baden-Baden, Nomos Verlagsgesellschaft.

Wentzel, Horst: 1997. "Philologie als Textwissenschaft. Alte und neue Horizonte. Einleitung", *Zeitschrift für Deutsche Philologie*, 116.

Wilken, Lisanne: 2001. *Enhed i Mangfoldighed?* Århus University Press.

Lotman, Bakhtin, and the Problem of a Semiotics of Culture

by
Jostein Børtnes

I should like to start by quoting a young Norwegian German scholar, Helge Jordheim, who recently referred to the "philological triad" or the "philological paradigm"(Jordheim 2001; 25–78). According to Jordheim, the philological paradigm, as people like Friedrich D. E. Schleiermacher and August Boeckh fleshed it out in the 19th century, comprised three perspectives, or approaches:

1. grammar, in its widest sense of the scientific study of language, comprising syntax and morphology, as well as what we today call phonology and semantics;
2. criticism, in the sense of textual criticism, and
3. hermeneutics, or the science of interpretation.

In other words, in the course of the 19th century, philology developed into an interpretive science comprising not only linguistics, but the study of history and literature as well. Philology combined linguistic analysis with a critical examination of the various layers of a text, and, finally, with a scholarly interpretation of its meaning and historical context.

Towards the end of the 19th century, however, this overarching paradigm fell apart into the isolated disciplines we know today: linguistics, textual criticism, history and literary studies. Historians were the first to break away, maintaining that history was a study of people and events of the past *outside* the body of inherited texts. Next came textual criticism, defined as a mechanic study of textual transmission as a mechanical process outside history. Linguistics followed suit, and when Ferdinand de Saussure's *Cours de linguistique générale* was published posthumously in 1916, its emphasis on the *synchronic* study of *la langue*, i. e. on the study of language in its systematic aspect at a particular period without considering its history, linguistics and philology, too, had parted ways. Only literary scholars still had – and have – to acquire the skills of philology in order to be able to read and understand the literary heritage.

Saussurian linguistics became known in Russia at the end of the First World War – first and foremost through Saussure's student, Serge Karcevski, during his short-lived return to Russia from Geneva in 1917–1919, when, according to Roman Jacobson, he "fired the young generation of Moscow linguists with the *Cours de linguistique générale* and applied its precepts to the study of contemporary Russian"(Jakobson 1971; 518).

In spite of their enthusiastic reception of the new linguistics, Roman Jakobson and his colleagues in the Moscow Linguistic Circle remained critical to a number of Saussure's central tenets. True, Jakobson followed Saussure in his emphasis on *opposition* and *system* as fundamental to a structural linguistics, and he joined him in defining language as a *system of signs*, as well as in placing linguistics within the framework of a general science of sign systems, a *semiology*, or *semiotics*. But Jakobson also disagreed with Saussure on a number of important points. First, he modified Saussure's theory of *l'arbitraire du signe*, the arbitrariness of the sign. Second, he criticised the other scholar's emphasis on the *linearity* of the sign, and, thirdly, he questioned a number of Saussure's oppositions, dichotomies representing different aspects of language which, according to the *Course*, in a scientific study of language must be kept separate: *langue* versus *parole*, *form* versus *substance*, the *systematic* versus the *associative* (later called the *paradigmatic*), and *synchrony* versus *diachrony*.

Jakobson accepted these oppositions, but maintained at the same time that they must be overcome in order to prevent the conception of language as a whole from falling apart. The opposition *langue–parole*, for instance, is described by Saussure as an opposition between system and application, between the social and the individual, *langue* being the genuine object of linguistics. Jakobson, on the other hand, claimed that one may also speak of an individual person's linguistic system, and that the application of language in speech presupposes at least two participants. The definition of *langue* as the social and *parole* as the individual therefore fails to convince, and, consequently, *langue* ought not to be studied apart from *parole*, but both in their interaction. In the second part of the last century, Jakobson substituted for *langue* and *parole* the less ambiguous terms "code" and "message", taken over from communication theory. Likewise, Jakobson replaced Saussure's opposition between the *syntagmatic* and the *paradigmatic* with "selection" and "combination" as the two fundamental aspects of language. By *form* and *substance* Saussure envisaged functions versus matter. Form structures linguistic matter in different ways in different languages. What matters in language is form: what is crucial is the difference between linguistic units. Linguistic units are oppositive, relative and negative.

Jakobson accepted the idea of linguistic units as oppositive and relative, but not as negative. Again, it is the interplay of form and substance that matters to him. The study of language is not a study of form alone. At the same time, Jakobson goes further than Saussure in emphasising the relativity of linguistic units. And by bringing out relative differences one is, according to Jakobson, able to define what they have in common, their invariant features. *Relational invariance* is fundamental to Jakobsons concept of language.

The most significant point in Jakobson's response to Saussure, however, is his critique of the latter's opposition between *synchronic* and *diachronic* linguistics, the description of language as a static system versus the description of linguistic change, which, according to Saussure, could only describe the diachronic development of individual elements, which by Saussure is defined as aimless and unrelated to the system. As early as in 1927, Jakobson distanced himself from this view, claiming that historical evolution must be described in terms of a system of different but interdependent elements. The evolution of language as a means of communication is neither blind nor accidental. Changes have a cause. They may, for instance, serve to restore the balance when the system has been destabilised. Besides, Jakobson refused to identify synchronic and diachronic with static and dynamic. The state of language at a given point in time is dynamic, too, involving, for instance, a dynamic tension between older and younger forms that are often used with different stylistic values.

In conclusion, we may say that whereas in Saussure oppositions are irreconcilable, Jakobson always strives to connect them, to see them as complementary. In contrast to many Western structuralists, whose aim it was to construct new theories and to introduce new concepts, emphasising discontinuity and difference, Jakobson consciously placed himself within the great tradition of Russian and Western European philological scholarship.

Turning now to Yurii Lotman and Mikhail Bakhtin, and the problems of a semiotics of culture, we should keep in mind that the former developed his ideas and theories on the basis of the Russian Formalists and Roman Jakobson, in contrast to the latter, whose ideas about literature and culture evolved in opposition to those propounded by Jakobson and the Formalists.

In his opening report at the First International Congress of Semiotics in Milan, 2 June 1974, "A Glance at the Development of Semiotics" (originally published in French as "Coup d'œil sur le développement de la sémiotique"), Jakobson indirectly refers to the Moscow-Tartu school of Yurii Lotman and Boris Uspensky when he says that "the confrontation of language with 'secondary modelling structures' and with mythology particularly points to a rich harvest and calls upon able minds to undertake an analogous type of work which attempts to embrace the semiotics of culture" (Jakobson 1985; 213f.).

Jakobson's "secondary modelling structures" is clearly a slightly inaccurate rendering of "secondary modelling system," a concept suggested by the brother of B. A. Uspensky, the mathematician V. A. Uspensky, and taken over by the Tartu semioticians, when, in the 1970s they advanced their study of a "semiotics of culture." In the "Theses on a Semiotic Study of Culture," published in 1973 and signed by B. A. Uspensky, V. V. Ivanov, V. N. Toporov, A. M. Pyatigorsky, and Yurii Lotman, we find the following definition:

> Under secondary modelling systems we understand such semiotic systems with the aid of which models of the world or its fragments are constructed. These systems are secondary in relation to the primary systems of natural language, over which they are built – directly (the supralinguistic system of literature), or in a shape parallel to it (music, painting). ("Theses": 6.1.0)

The concept of culture underlying this definition, is given in the opening paragraph of the "Theses":

> In the study of culture the initial premise is that all human activity concerned with the processing, exchange and storage of information possesses a certain unity. Individual sign systems, though presupposing immanently organised structures, function only in unity, supported by each other. None of the sign systems possesses a mechanism which would enable it to function culturally in isolation. Hence it follows that, together with an approach which permits us to construct a number of relatively autonomous sciences of the semiotic cycle, we shall admit another approach, according to which all of them examine particular aspects of the *semiotics of culture*, of the study of the functional correlation of different sign systems. ("Theses" 1.0.0)

Crucial to this definition of culture is the theory that any culture presupposes pairs of correlated semiotic systems: "the pursuit of heterogeneity of languages is a characteristic feature of culture" ("Theses" 6.1.0). Both in the "Theses" and in other writings, Lotman is very much concerned with the tension between different sign systems. The opposition between discrete (verbal) and non-discrete (visual or iconic) texts, for example, "constitutes one of the most permanent mechanisms of culture as a whole" ("Theses" 3.2.1). Such oppositions are described as playing a special role in the system of culture generating semiotic oppositions, since each type needs the other "in order to form the mechanism of culture." But each type also needs to be different "according to the principle of semiosis, that is to say, on the one hand equivalent, and on the other hand not entirely mutually convertible" ("Theses" 6.2.0). This last formulation became central to Lotman's investigations into the semiotics of culture in the 80s and 90s.

From the very beginning, Saussure's opposition between *langue* and *parole*, between *synchrony* and *diachrony* has run the risk of becoming an opposition between the abstract and the concrete, between the static and the dynamic. In the 1970s, this problem gave rise to a debate in social anthropology in which it was argued that by "decoding," i. e. abstracting the code from the message, we necessarily reduce and lose the level of meaning.[1] According to Irene Portis Winner, a number of distinguished anthropologists, Clifford Geertz and Victor Turner among them, maintained that structuralists "consider the discovery of an elementary structure as an explanation and interpretation of the phenomenon itself." The implicit assumption is "that symbol systems are necessarily consistent and unchanging and therefore cannot express multivocal, complex, ambiguous and conflicting reality" (Winner 1978; 352f.).

Looking back from our own vantage point, we can now see that what this debate really was about was the opposition between closed and open systems. In the West, semiotic systems were often as a matter of course regarded as closed, while for Lotman, as for Western anthropologists such as Lévi-Strauss and Edmund Leach, structures are, as Irene Portis Winner observes, "organized by both conflict and harmony, not closed, and in a constant process of change characterized by the inseparable process of incorporating new, even antithetical, elements and by transformation. Structures are never to be understood as separate from context and are not purely cognitive, but unite emotive, aesthetic and cognitive functions in ever-changing hierarchies. Thus, such structures encompass an inseparable whole the concrete and the abstract, *langue* and *parole* or competence and performance" (Winner 1978, 354.).

Already in an article from 1974, later reprinted several times, "Dinamicheskaya model' semioticheskoi sistemy,'" Lotman broached the general problems indicated by Irene Portis Winner in the passage quoted above. And he was to come back to them in many different ways in the following decades, notably in his book in English, *Universe of the Mind* (1990), where a whole section is devoted to "Cultural Memory, History and Semiotics." Here he explicitly refers to the work of Ilya Prirogine and Isabella Stengers on dynamic and irreversible processes and their implications for history (Lotman 197 & 1990, 230-232).

Referring back to the work of Roman Jakobson and the Prague school, Yurii Tynyanov and Bakhtin, however, Lotman in the 1974 article acknowledges the methodological merit of the synchrony-diachrony opposition, arguing, as Irene Portis Winner puts it, that the distinction is of a relative and heuristic, rather than of an existential nature. In the evolution of a system, these two categories interpenetrate. Lotman speaks of their "vzai-

---

[1] For this debate, see Irene Portis Winner 1978; 352.

moperekhodimost", their "interpervasion"(Lotman 1992; 91). In a dynamic model of a semiotic system there are a number of antinomies that a static system ignores, the most important being that between the systematic, i. e. "those system elements and their relationships that remain invariant throughout any homomorphous transformation," and the extra-systematic, those elements that are marked by their instability and irregularity, and which in a static, closed system may be defined as nonexistent or as allosystemic. In an analysis of dynamic systems antinomies such as these cannot be neutralised, but have to be included in the description as "features of the dynamic state of a semiotic system, its immanent semiotic mechanisms which allow it, while changing with the changing social context, to preserve homeostasis, i. e. to remain itself" (Lotman 1992; 101).

An important aspect of the Moscow-Tartu theory of a semiotics of culture is the concept of text. Already in the "Theses" of 1973 culture is defined "as a hierarchy of semiotic systems composed of texts, as the sum of the texts and the set of functions correlated with them, or as a certain mechanism which generates these texts" (Theses 6.0.0).

Chapter 15 of *The Universe of the Mind*, "Historical laws and the structure of text," is one of many places where Lotman returns to and develops his concept of text and its significance for the study of history. The chapter does, in fact, open with the sweeping statement that "The historian has to deal with texts." And he continues to claim that the historian "cannot observe events, but acquires narratives of them from written sources" (Lotman 1990; 221). This may sound self-evident, until we remember that the objective of modern historiography has been to go beyond the text in order to establish "wie es wirklich gewesen." However, Lotman's approach is in several ways related to Paul de Man's deconstructive philology and to Louis A. Montrose's "new historicism". The return to philology advocated by de Man in his essay of that title, as well as in his "Literary history and literary modernity," means that "the bases for historical knowledge are not empirical facts but written texts, even if these texts masquerade in the guise of wars and revolutions" (de Man 1983; 165). Montrose, in his article, "Professing the Renaissance: The Poetics and Politics of Culture," defines his post-structuralist approach to history as the "reciprocal interest in the textuality of history and the historicity of the text"(Montrose 1989; 20).

Yet, Lotman goes further and in a different direction. In his critique of historians who in the past "sometimes drew a distinction between information derived from written sources, which was felt to be ambivalent and in need of interpretation, and the irrefutable evidence of material culture, archaeological data and iconic depictions," he asserts that "from the point of view of semiotics these are all texts and all share the consequences of using a text as medium, so the question of the influence of the text on historical knowledge cannot be avoided:

> The transformation of an event into a text involves, first, narrating it in the system of a particular language, i. e. subjecting it to a previously given structural organization. The event itself may seem to the viewer (or participant) to be disorganized (chaotic) or to have an organization that is beyond the field of interpretation, or indeed to be an accumulation of several discrete structures. But when an event is retold by means of a language then it inevitably acquires a structural unity. This unity, which in fact belongs only to the expression level, inevitably becomes transferred to the level of content too. So the very fact of transforming an event into a text raises the degree of its organization. Besides, the interpreter invariably applies to the real-life associations of the event the system of associations in the language . . . [T]he very necessity that compels the historian to rely on texts, and compels the texts to narrate the events according to the laws of linguistic, logical, rhetorical and narrative constructions, means that historical reality reaches the historian in a form he [or she] knows is distorted. On top of this is the ideological encoding which is hierarchically the highest stage in the construction of the narrative text: it includes the genre code as well as political, social, religious and philosophical ones." (Lotman 1990, 221-223)

But in addition to the deformation which non-textual reality undergoes when it is turned into the text which is the historian's primary material, Lotman points to another source of deformation of reality which is not related to the author of the text, but to the interpretation of the historian when he looks at history. For history "develops along a time-vector: its course is defined by the movement from the past to present; but a historian looks at the texts from the present to the past":

> For the majority of authors who have studied the epistemology of historical science, the identity of the forward-looking and the retrospective points of view has been a self-evident truth and the question has not even been taken into account. They believed that the essence of the chain of events did not alter whether we look at them in the direction of the time vector or from the opposite point of view. Indeed, for those who regard history as a movement towards a certain goal, this view seems a natural one. (Lotman 1990; 229)

Discussing Marc Bloch's belief that the retrospective view allows the historian to distinguish the essential from the accidental, Lotman argues that "if we start from the premise that an historical event is always the result of one of many possible alternatives and that the same conditions do not always produce the same results," we have to use other methods: "we shall see that the events which actually took place are surrounded by clusters of unrealized possibilities." What the retrospective view neglects, is the fact that history is "an irreversible (unbalanced) process" (Lotman 1990, 230).

It is at this point of his discussion Lotman introduces the work of Ilya Prirogine and Isabella Stengers on such processes. According to the two researchers, dynamic processes behave differently in different areas. Occurring in conditions of equilibrium they follow predetermined curves. But the further they move from the points of equilibrium, the closer the movement comes to "those critical points at which the predictable course of the processes breaks off." Prirogine and Stengers call them "bifurcation points": "at these points the process reaches a point when clear predictability of the future is no longer possible. The next stage comes by the realization of one of several equally probable alternatives." Quoting Isaiah Berlin on the difference between the natural and the humanitarian sciences as a difference between interest in the repeatable and interest in the unique – i. e. between the *nomothetic* and the *idiographic* – Prirogine and Stengers observe that "When we move from equilibrium to far-from-equilibrium conditions we move away from the repetitive and the universal to the specific and the unique." "In extreme conditions of disequilibrium the processes flow not in a smooth predetermined course, but they fluctuate." When fluctuation occurs "at the right moment" this results in "favouring one reaction path over a number of other equally possible paths":

> Self-organization processes in far-from-equilibrium conditions correspond to a delicate interplay between chance and necessity, between fluctuations and deterministic laws. We expect that near a bifurcation, fluctuations or random elements would play an important role, while between bifurcations the deterministic aspects would become dominant. (Lotman 1990, 231-2)

According to Lotman, Prirogine and Stengers' ideas about dynamic processes can also be applied to history. But at the same time, another factor has to be taken into account. For historical development takes place with interference from "individuals endowed with intelligence and freedom," and this means that "at the bifurcation points what comes into action is not only the mechanism of chance but also the mechanism of *conscious choice* and this becomes the most important *objective* factor in the historical process" (Lotman 1990; 232). At moments of bifurcation, Prirogine explains, "the process acquires individuality taking on the characteristics of a human being" (Lotman 1990, 233).

In history, bifurcation points are

> moments when the behaviour of individuals and the masses ceases to be automatically predictable and determinacy recedes to the background. At these moments the movement of history should be pictured not as a trajectory but as a continuum that is potentially capable of resolving itself into any number of variants. These nodal points with diminished predictability are times of revolution or other dramatic historical shifts. The choice that will be realized, depends on a complex of chance circumstances, but even more on the self-awareness of the people involved. This is why at such times speech, discourse, propaganda have especially great historical *significance. And if* before the choice was made the situation was unpredictable, *after* the choice

has been made the situation is one that in principle is a new one, a situation for which the choice was essential, and which in the future course of history will seem to have been inevitable. The choice, which was open to chance before, seems predetermined *afterwards*. A retrospective view intensifies determinacy and for the future course of history that choice will seem like the first link in a new law of history. (Lotman 1990, 233)

Quoting Prirogine to the effect that "at the moments of bifurcation the process acquires individuality taking on the characteristics of a human being," Lotman proposes a way to chart the degrees of intensity of unpredictability: "the interference of chance – the interference of a thinking being – the interference of a creative consciousness:

If at one pole of the historical process there is iron determinacy, at the other there is creative (artistic) creativity. Neither pole is to be found in pure form in the actual process. But we can demonstrate the isomorphism of these processes at different levels by pointing to a work of art which *before* its creation is unpredictable and *afterwards* seems like the predetermined beginning of a predestined tradition." (Lotman 1990; 233)

The problem of the individual is particularly important in history seen in terms of a dynamic process, since the process of history is never wholly predictable, but implies acts of choice between equal alternatives. And, as Lotman comments, "consciousness is always a choice," and "if we exclude choice (unpredictability which the outside observer sees as chance) then we exclude consciousness from the historical process. And historical laws are different from all others in that they cannot be understood without taking account of people's conscious activity, including semiotic activity" (Lotman 1990, 234).

It is interesting to compare Lotman's discussions of the semiotics of culture in the 70s and 80s with the opinion expressed by the American anthropologist Marshal Sahlins in a retrospective glance at social anthropology during the last two decades of the last century. According to T. M. Luhrman, Sahlins now maintains that one of the most challenging problems in social anthropology of the last two decades has been the problem of history, i. e. "the relationship between the organising patterns of culture and the actions of individuals, between structure and events." In his attempt to solve this problem, Sahlins claims that "there is at best an analytic, and certainly not an actual, distinction between structure and event, because circumstances are always recognised through cultural idioms and those idioms never stand free of specific moments, places and people." Moreover, he argues that "no matter how powerful and constraining the cultural patterns, history is always chaotic – in the now technical sense of the word" (Luhrman 2001; 8).

At this point, I should like to move a step further, now in the direction of Bakhtin and the impact of his thought on cultural semiotics. But I want to approach Bakhtin by way of a quick look at the American anthropologist Lars Rodseth's distributive model of culture, in which Bakhtin plays a crucial role (Rodseth 1998).

At the beginning of his argument, Rodseth refers to the concept of a *distributive* model of culture, proposed by Theodore Schwartz in 1978. This model "construes culture not as an integrated system or text and not as a mere aggregation of traits of behaviors but as a semantic population – a population of meanings":

> These meanings have definite material embodiments. They may be stored in human brains, expressed in speech and other forms of action, or transmitted in writing or other artefacts, but they are always things in the world rather than mere abstractions. (Rodseth 1998; 55)

According to this view, meanings are not to be found "in formal or idealised systems but in spatiotemporal distributions which may or may not be orderly, coherent, or stable." With a reference to the anthropologist Dan Sperber, Rodseth maintains that a relatively widespread and enduring distribution can be usefully described as a population, a term, however, that does not imply that cultures are neatly bounded or continuous entities. Quite on the contrary: the concept of population is "precisely suited to phenomena that vary, interact, reproduce, and spread – living things, in short, as opposed to abstract or inanimate objects" (Rodseth 1998; 55).

Now, to treat meanings as living things would from a modern anthropologist's point of view seem absurd. But, and this is the point where Bakhtin enters the discussion, with his conception of semantic forms as dynamic, metamorphic, and interactive, Rodseth finds support for his distributive model for instance in the following passage:

> The living word . . . enters a dialogically agitated and tension-filled environment of alien words, value judgements and accents, weaves in and out of complex interrelationships, merges with some and recoils from others, intersects with yet a third group: and all this crucially shapes discourse. . . . [Thus] the living utterance, having taken meaning and shape at a particular historical moment in a socially specific environment, cannot fail to brush up against thousands of living dialogic threads. (Bakhtin; 1981, 276)

In Bakhtin's perspective, meanings are, as Rodseth stresses, not just living, but social things, interacting and recombining "to create flowing macroentities, which we recognize as cultural forms" (Rodseth 1998; 56). And he quotes Michel Foucault to the effect that "a science, or novels or political speeches, or the oeuvre of an author, or even a single book" should be approached from the outset as "a population of events" – that is "a finite grouping" of statements, spoken or written, in a given time and place, drawing the conclusions that such groupings are "not essences, structures, or types, but specific sets of things in the world" (Rodseth 1998, 56). This leads over into "the well-established viewpoint of population biology" and the fact that, according to Michael Ghiselin, "biology has ceased to think in terms of abstract classes or idealized forms such as 'the horse' and has turned to considering the interactions between 'this horse' and 'that horse' emphasising the uniqueness and dynamism of every living thing. This is modern biology's alternative to essentialism, i.e. the view that reality consists of unchanging essences or types underlying the variable and accidental features of the world.[2] Semantic populations, then, are like biological populations, consisting of unique and changeable entities. Even a given word may be defined as such a "living multitude of meaning and accent". Seen in this perspective, Rodseth argues, we no longer have to conceive of cultures as *either* "natural objects" or "things," *or* ongoing semiotic processes, as claimed by Richard Handler and others. The distinction between things and processes, Rodseth alleges, "might as easily be viewed as a contrast between inanimate objects and living populations, which exhibit precisely the kind of fluidity and changeability that Handler takes to be the hallmark of cultures. From a populational perspective, cultures are both 'natural' *and* 'semiotic'" (Rodseth 1998; 65, n.1).

In Bakhtin, who, by the way never saw himself as a semiotician, and who, in my opinion, should not be regarded as one by us either, words and their meanings are unique to every single person. In his dialogic world, no two speakers use the same language in exactly the same way. Every utterance, therefore, is a unique event; not an objective thing, but a living entity, authored by a living subject, and therefore itself a subject. This means, that the human sciences are not dealing with objects, but with other subjects. We experience this most clearly with works of art and literature, but it also, I think, holds true for other cultural utterances, or texts. This subjectivity implies that cultural components like components of language are variously distributed among the individual utterances and their authors. Every member of a cultural carries but his or her unique fragment of the whole. Culture as open and dynamic knowledge systems may be reconceptualised as variable and interactive populations of meanings, a concept that differs radically from concepts that, as Rodseth reminds us, "stress sharing within cultures and boundaries between cultures" (Rodseth 1998, 56).

References

[2] Rodseth 1998, 56, quoting Ernst Mayr, *The Growth of Biological Thought: Diversity, Evolution, and Inheritance*, Cambridge, MA: Harvard University press, 1982, and Karl R. Popper, *Conjectures and Refutations*, New York: Basic Books, 1962.

Bakhtin, Mikhail M.: 1981. *The Dialogic Imagination: Four Essays by M. M. Bakhtin*, ed. Michael Holquist. Austin, University of Texas Press, 276.

de Man, Paul: 1983. "Literary history and literary modernity," *Blindness and Insight*. New York, Oxford University Press, 1971, rev. ed. London, Methuen & Co., pp. 142–165, 165.

Jordheim, Helge: 2001. *Lesningens vitenskap: utkast til en ny filologi*, Oslo, Universitetsforlaget.

Jakobson, Roman: 1971. "Sergej Karcevskij: August 28, 1884 – November 7, 1955," *Selected Writings*, 2. The Hague; Paris, Mouton, pp. 517–521, 518.

– 1985. "A Glance at the Development of Semiotics," *Selected Writings*, VII, Berlin; New York; Amsterdam, Mouton, pp. 199–218, 213 f.

Lotman, Yurii: 1973. "Tezisy k semioticheskomu izucheniyu kul'tur: (V primenenii k slavyanskim tekstam)," *Semiotyka i struktura tekstu*, ed. M. R. Mayenowa. Warszawa, PAN, pp. 9–32.

– 1974. "Dinamicheskaya model' semioticheskoi sistemy," Moscow (Inst. rus. yaz. AN SSSR, probl. gruppa po eksperim. i priklad. lingvistike, predvar. publ., vyp. 60).

– 1990. *Universe of the Mind*, London & New York, Tauris & Co., pp. 230–232. (Russ. version, *Vnurti myslyashchikh mirov*, Moscow: Yazyki russkoi kul'tury, 1996, pp. 321–323).

– 1991. "Dinamicheskaya model' semioticheskoi sistemy," *Izbarannye stat'i*, 1. Tallin, "Aleksandra," pp. 90–101, 91.

Luhrman, T. M.: 2001. "The Culture Club," TLS, 8 June, 7-8. (Review of Adam Kuper, *Culture: The anthropologist's account*, and Marshall Sahlins, *Culture in Practice: Selectd essays*.)

Mayr, Ernst: 1982. *The Growth of Biological Thought: Diversity, Evolution, and Inheritance*. Cambridge, MA, Harvard University press.

Montrose, Louis A.: 1989. "Professing the Renaissance: The Poetics and Policies of Culture," ed. H. Aram Veeser, *The New Historicism*. New York & London, Routledge, pp. 15–37, 20.

Popper, Karl R.: 1962. *Conjectures and Refutations*. New York, Basic Books.

Rodseth, Lars: 1998. "Distributive Models of Culture: A Sapirian Alternative to Essentialism," *American Anthropologist*, 100 /1, pp. 55–69.

Schwartz, Theodore: 1978. "Where is the Culture? Personality as the Distributive Locus of Culture," *The Making of Psychological Anthropology*, ed. George D. Spindler. Berkeley, University of California Press, pp. 419–441.

Winner, Irene Portis: 1978. "Cultural Semiotics and Anthropology," *The Sign: Semiotics around the world*, ed. R. W. Bailey, L. Matejka & P. Steiner. Ann Arbor, The University of Michigan, 1978, pp. 335-363, 352.

The Relation between Micro- and Macropragmatics in Modern Language Studies

by

Jacob L. Mey

University of Southern Denmark

1. Introduction: The split

Let me begin by recounting a personal experience. As a young student of linguistics at the University of Copenhagen, I was trained in the tradition of the time, in a wide array of philological disciplines. When I prepared for my final exams, I counted the languages I had studied, and came up with the astonishing number of 25! These languages included not only the "classical" ones, Greek, Latin, and Sanskrit, but also most of the other languages belonging to the Indo-European family, plus a couple-three outside of that family (such as Finnish or Greenlandic). All of this was prescribed in exact wording by the regulations for the study of general linguistics, and the exams were conducted in the traditional way of written translation followed by an oral examination on the text (either familiar or new). When it came to my exam in Sanskrit, I was given a text from the Ṛg-Veda to read and comment. It was the famous hymn to Indra from the first book, the one that begins with the words: "I will now praise the manly deeds of Indra..." (*Indrasya nu vīryāṇ i pra vocaṃ* ...; RV I; 36). At a certain point in this hymn, an allusion is made to a sacrificial bench, on which the priest is to perform his tribute to the god. I was able to translate this term correctly, but one of the three examiners, the professor of Sanskrit himself, was not quite satisfied with my just giving a translation. He wanted to know in more detail what this bench was made of, and how the sacrifice was performed. I was not familiar with all those details, having read the text purely as an exercise in the Vedic language (even though until this very moment, the beauty of the hymn still holds its sway). At this point, the head examiner, my own professor of linguistics (the famous Louis Hjelmslev) intervened and told his colleague that such questions were outside of what one could expect the candidate to know, and so I was spared further cross-examination. (I also passed).

Now what is the point of telling this anecdote in the context of our theme: changing philologies? In the wording of the conveners of this conference, we are faced with the demise of a paradigm, so deeply ingrained in the philologies of the past, a paradigm which had as its object the indivisible unity of culture and life, including language. "Philology is determined by its object, the culture ... this culture is a unity", just as "life itself is a unity; and because of this, so is our science" (Wilamowitz-Moellendorff 1921; 1; cit. Benne 2001; 23). My Sanskrit professor was right, being a philologist, in asking me about the signification of an element of culture, as it was represented in the language; he believed strongly in the unity of the language and of the life that it represented. In contrast, my own professor, who was a linguist, advocated the study of language as an independent, even "immanent" discipline (Hjelmslev 1943; 3); for him, the question of what the words meant, in the context of life, was only secondary to the question of how these words entered into the system of the languages that he studied.

I have often thought back to this episode as emblematic for the difference between old-fashioned philology and what we as students used to call the "new" linguistics. To quote Hjelmslev's own, ironic bon-mot, "a good linguist doesn't need to know many (or even any) languages" – a saying that became classic, even though its source was a living testimony to the contrary, inasmuch as Hjelmslev spoke at least seven languages fluently. But by his attitude, which he passed on to his students, he represented, more than anyone else, the split between the analytic linguist, who studies the system of language, and the traditional philologist, who tries to understand a text and interpret it as an expression of the life of humans.

The next sections will elucidate the origins and consequences of this split. Following that, I will comment on how it affects our understanding of language studies, and in particular of what a future 'philology' might look like.

2. Saussure and the consequences
2.1. Hjelmslev.
Ferdinand de Saussure, often called 'the father of modern linguistics', defined linguistics as the study of *langue*, the system of language, in contrast to that which is actually said, *parole*. (1949; 37ff). For Saussure, *parole* is the entirety of what people say ("la somme de ce que les gens disent", ibid.; 38); this summation is nevertheless done on an individual basis: there is nothing social in people's speech ("il n'y a rien de collectif dans la parole", ibid.) And Saussure concludes his chapter 4 of the *Cours* with the words "We will concentrate exclusively on the latter [that is to say, linguis-

tics proper, JM], the linguistics that has langue as its proper object" (ibid.; 39) – even to the extent that he doesn't want to recognize a "linguistique de la parole".[1]

So there we are. The Saussurean split is complete, and it was going to be perfected in the linguistic theories that have flourished during the past century. I want only to mention one among the many that may be caught under the common hat of 'structuralism': the theory developed by the Danish post-Saussurean Louis Hjelmslev under the appellation of 'glossematics'. In this theory, the language is defined as a system, to which there corresponds a process; the system is necessary, the process is not. If we found somewhere on another planet a language which was totally different from any language spoken on our planet, but which had, for instance, the same system as does Latin, then that language would be Latin, Hjelmslev used to say, using a favorite example of his.

Philology, for Hjelmslev, is thus a kind of non-science (not to say nonsense, in the strict sense of the word). As he says, in his best-known work, the *Prolegomena* (1943), when it comes to philology, it is "an illusion to believe that one is studying language itself: it is not the language itself, but the *disiecta membra* of the language, that do not offer the possibility of comprehending the totality that language represents; [it is] the physical and physiological, psychological and logical, sociological and historical residues of language [that one studies], not language itself." (1943; 7 – my translation).

The so-called 'residues' that Hjelmslev dismisses here in such a perfunctory way are precisely the elements of the language that come to the fore when we study texts, not only as linguistic specimina attesting to the existence of certain language-internal structures (typically, the sentences used in linguistic textbooks, for the majority fabricated by the linguists themselves), but as part of the speaking person's *parole*. Texts represent words that come out of a living person's mind and body, not out of the schematic representations à la the 'talking heads' that Saussure was the first to introduce in his Cours ("deux personnes, A et B, qui s'entretiennent"; 1949; 27). It is from the minds and mouths of real, live speakers, not from the schematized representations favored by linguists and other theoreticians, that the study of language as a social phenomenon takes its beginning. It is also here that a true integration of the disciplines dealing with language in some way or other (that is to say, not just with *langue*, but with language as it is used in society) can take place.

---

[1] Even though Saussure himself opens up for the possibility of a "linguistique de la parole" (albeit with much reserve: "on peut parler", "à la rigueur", 1949; 38), his translators note that "F. de Sausssure n'a jamais abordé dans ses leçons la linguistique de la parole" (ibid. 197) – and for a reason, as we have seen.

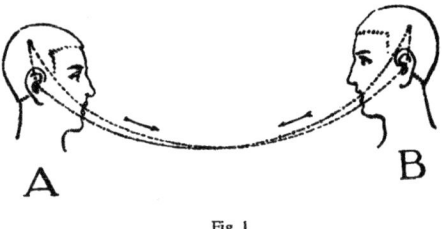

Fig. 1

Saussure's 'Talking Heads'

(*Cours de linguistique générale*, Paris 1916, p. 27)

2.2. Bakhtin.

Interestingly, more or less at the same time that Hjelmslev was speculating about language as a system that "rested in itself", with its own laws and structures (cf. 1943; 7), a contemporary of his, but unbeknownst to Hjelmslev, was grappling with the same post-Saussurean legacy. Reflecting on Dostoyevsky's *Notes from Underground*, the Russian linguist and semiotician Mikhail M. Bakhtin comments on the latter's vision of a "table of logarithms" to be drawn up to explain the details of our existence down to the minutest of events (Dostoyevsky 1965; 30-31).[2] Here, Bakhtin might as well have chosen to contemplate Hjelmslev's speculations about a linguistic algebra, a "calculus, that will enable us to implement the tools to be used in describing and understanding a text and the language it is built upon" (1943; 17 – my translation). But contrary to the latter, he resolves the Saussurean dichotomy in favor of parole, the utterance, rather than in favor of a system of logical relations parading as langue, with sentences modeled on propositions.

Not surprisingly, contrary to Hjelmslev and other formalists, Bakhtin is aware of the dangers that are inherent in the concept of 'laws' and systems that try to subsume the linguistic phenomena as mere realizations of the laws – laws that are valid not just for the phenomena under observation but for all those that are possible, but not yet realized, and maybe not even realizable (cf. 1941; 17). What falls outside of the system, the actual utterances, transcends our descriptive schemata and is reduced to the status of 'residue': "the residue becomes a mere assembly of accidental, incomprehensible, unclassifiable phenomena" (Morson & Emerson 1990; 39); in other words, precisely what Hjelmslev, using an identical wording ("resi-

---

[2] "All human actions, by the same token, will then be calculated according to those laws [of nature, JM], in a mathematical fashion, like in a table of logarithms, up to 108,000, and recorded in the almanac; ..." (Dostoyevsky 1965; 30 – my translation).

dues"; in Danish: "udfældninger"; 1943; 7) so categorically dismissed when he talked about the psychological, physiological, sociological and other aspects that are by definition relegated outside the system of the language itself. As Morson & Emerson remark, in their ground-breaking study on Bakhtin:

> In Bakhtin's view, when Saussure abstracted *langue* from *parole*, the remainder, *parole*, could only be an accessory phenomenon, a formless realm outside scientific inquiry. Laws and residues are twin consequences of an untenable style of thought. (ibid.)

3. The problem of the other

Let's go back for a moment to the familiar drawing of what I (somewhat irreverently) have called 'Saussure's Talking heads'. Notice first that Saussure apparently only is interested in 'what comes out of the mouth', as the Bible has it (St. Matth. 15; 11). True, he has another person there as well, a listener; after all, the talks about two persons having a conversation. But what happens to this other person? He (he IS a male) only functions as a temporary receptacle for the speaker's "acte individuel" (1949; 27). As soon as the speaker is finished, the hearer becomes a speaker himself, and produces his own individual act of speaking (I'll come back to this aspect of 'acting' below, section 4.3).

However, the communication between A and B (if one can call it that) not only happens exclusively between the 'heads', with complete disregard for the body as a whole (I'll say more on the aspect of embodiment later, section 5), but in addition, the contact between the two speakers is thought of as a series of individual acts, with speakers producing sentences on their own, without concern for the rest of society. True, Saussure, in the sequel, admonishes us that "we must move beyond the individual act, which is only the embryo of language, and approach the social facts" (ibid.; 29 – my translation); but for him, this social fact ("le fait social") is only represented by the system of the language, *langue*, whereas the actual act of speaking, *parole*, only functions in an ancillary quality, "to shed light on the study of *langue*" (ibid.; 39).

In contrast, for those working in the Bakhtinian tradition, the separation of the 'social fact' of communication into roles such as 'speaker' and 'listener' is a priori vitiated by the individualistic warp that affects most of 20th century linguistics. Let me quote from Bakhtin's important essay, 'The Problem of Speech Genres', in which he discusses precisely the same passage from Saussure's Cours that I highlighted above.

> Still current in linguistics are such fictions as the "listener" and "understander" (partners of the "speaker"), ... These fictions produce a completely distorted idea of the complex and multifaceted process of active speech communication. Courses in general linguistics (even serious ones like Saus-

> sure's) frequently present graphic-schematic depictions of the two partners in speech communication – the speaker and the listener (who perceives the speech) – and provide diagrams of the active speech processes of the speaker and the corresponding passive processes of the listener's perception and understanding of the speech One cannot say that these diagrams are false or that they do not correspond to certain aspects of reality. But when they are put forth as the actual whole of speech communication, they become a scientific fiction. The fact is that when the listener perceives and understands the meaning (the language meaning) of speech, he simultaneously takes an active, responsive attitude toward it. ... Any understanding of live speech a live utterance, is inherently responsive, ... Any understanding is imbued with response and necessarily elicits it in one form or another. (1994; 68)

And Bakhtin concludes that

> The desire to make one's speech understood is only an abstract aspect of the speaker's concrete and total speech plan. Moreover, any speaker is himself a respondent to a greater or lesser degree. He is not, after all, the first speaker, the one who disturbs the eternal silence of the universe. and he presupposes not only the existence of the language system he is using [cf. Hjelmslev's idea of the system being presupposed by the process, 1943; 10-11; my addition, JM], but also the existence of preceding utterances – his own and others' – with which his given utterance enters into one kind of relation or another. (ibid.; 69)

What we should learn from this passage is simply this: In my speaking, I am no "Biblical Adam" (ibid.; 94), inventorying and naming things and distributing their appellations throughout the universe. My speaking has been pre-formed by the speakers and listeners before me, by the speech community of which I am a part. And it is already 'post-formed' towards the others, my future respondent(s).

Elsewhere, Bakhtin talks about this in term of 'dialogicity'; I would go one step further and call the speech process a *dialectic* one, inasmuch as my speech is totally dependent on the others' speech for its very existence; my speaking invokes the others' speaking in order to be spoken. Cf.:

> The role of the others for whom the utterance is constructed is extremely great. ... the role of these others, for whom my thought becomes actual thought for the first time (and thus also for my own self as well) is not that of passive listeners, but of active participants in speech communication.

Bakhtin echoes here a view of language use that had already been foreshadowed in the work of Marx and Engels, where they characterize language as "practical consciousness" (1974; 51) – a notion which I have further developed in my 1985 book by explicitating the interaction of practice and consciousness as a dialectic movement, "by which the consciousness of our societal praxis turns into a societal praxis of consciousness. This consciousness-praxis we call language" (Mey 1985; 219). For Bakhtin, the dialectics of communication is present as an "essential (constitutive) marker of the utterance .. its quality of being directed to someone, its addressivity" (ibid.; 95). The fact that an utterance is always addressed to someone, always 'turning to' another member of the community (Bakhtin used the Russian verb *obratit'sja* 'to turn to', in order to form the technical term *obraščennost'* for this quality), is that without which "the utterance does not and cannot exist" (ibid.; 99).

The significance of this viewpoint becomes clear when we consider the developments that have accompanied and accelerated the gradual demise of the structuralist paradigm during the second half of the last century: first of all, the rise of the discipline called pragmatics.

4. Pragmatics to the rescue!
4.1. Micropragmatics: From the inside out.
Bakhtin's critique of the Saussurean dichotomy concentrated on one aspect of the 'talking heads' model: the fact that it basically represents a monologic, at most doubly monologic, view of the communication process. Another aspect of the Saussurean doctrine went unnoticed much longer, at least in the West; it was the horror of anything that could not be strictly formalized. The models of linguistic thought that were in demand during the first half of the century found their inspiration (often explicitly) in the schools of thinking that consciously distanced themselves from anything that had to do with the 'meaning' of an utterance or sentence. Bloomfield's 1933 book *Language*, for many the epitome of linguistic thinking, devotes only a very short chapter to this subject, and basically concludes that, since we cannot formalize meaning, we had best leave it alone. And Hjelmslev, in his *Prolegomena*, reflects this attitude in his wish to formalize meaning in such a way that it completely parallels form; as a consequence, meaning (or 'purport') cannot be described in his system except on a rather rudimentary level of abstraction. Hjelmslev, too, acknowledges his debt to the so-called 'Neopositivist' schools of thinking, first of all the Vienna Circle philosophers Neurath and Carnap and their Danish counterparts such as Jørgen Jørgensen. In the US, a man called Chomsky had a resounding success by preconizing the basically mathematical structure of the language system, conceived of as an exercise in grammatical derivation, practiced in parallel to the derivation of well-formed formulas in logic and of theorems in mathematics.

While all this was going on, and almost behind of the back of the theorizing linguists, some people in England had started to 'colonize' the shores of meaning, as Leech colorfully expressed it (1983; 2; Mey 2001; 21). The metaphor is apt, even though, as Leech also points out, those shores were by no means empty spaces: there were traces in the sand not just of one, but of many philosophical savages who had cultivated the land for many years and had produced an interesting bunch of results that either were unknown to the linguists or – if they were confronted with them – were dismissed by the latter as not 'linguistic'.[3]

Also, one should not confound the 'colonization' that was going on here with the work of the homesteading philosophers. The linguists extended their familiar paradigms to comprise larger and larger units in a motion one could call 'centrifugal'; in contrast, some at least of the philosophers worked from the outside in, centripetally, so to speak, by steadily refining and more narrowly defining some global insights they had obtained. (I will come back to this division below).

In this connection, the fact that a philosopher like John Austin could raise the question what one could do with one's language, rather than just describe it and be done, was one that deserved to be taken seriously also in a linguistic context. Unfortunately, the linguists of the times, being mired in their syntax-only views, were unable to absorb these new insights, that had to be introduced by the back door, so to speak. The way this was done was in the guise of the theory of *speech acts*.

Speech act theory, as originally propounded by Austin and refined by mainly Grice and Searle in the sixties and seventies, turned the linguistic paradigm on its head. Rather than raising byzantine questions about correctness and well-formedness (Chomsky's 'derivation'), Austin considered the true problem to be the question what an utterance could bring about of effects in the 'real' world. Rather than saying something about an imperative or a question being well-formed, hence 'in the language', the speech act theorists wanted to know how this particular imperative or question functioned in a context of activity, and how the effects of the act were obtained (or not, as the case might be: the case of 'misfiring', in Austin's picturesque terminology).

And here, it turned out to be the case that what was said sometimes was not so important as that which was not. The Berkeley philosopher Paul Grice made his philosophical fortune by pointing out that in order to be effective, a speech act needn't be explicit, but could leave things unsaid: namely, when what is unsaid but could have been said, is understood as a much stronger statement than if the unsaid (and sometimes unsayable) had been said directly, as when the then Cardinal-Archbishop of Paris, Mgr Emmanuel Suhard, was asked about his opinion of Charles de Gaulle, even before the latter came to power in 1958. The Prince of the Church replied very diplomatically by saying: 'He is a very good Catholic' – implying all sorts of unsaid and in fact unsayable things about the great politician which he, as a Catholic Church dignitary known for his rather tepid

---

[3] In the words of one famous linguist of the Chomsky school who, when asked about his opinion of the 1969 Searle work on *Speech Acts* remarked that it probably wasn't linguistically oriented, hence of little interest.

political attitudes, and one who certainly was not a 'gaulliste', would and could not bring himself to utter.

All these efforts to expand the framework of linguistic studies, respectively to draw language into a study of human activity, remained confined mostly to the realm of what used to be called the 'proposition' by logicians and philosophers, the 'sentence' by linguists. As we have just seen, the tradition championed by the Bakhtinians resolved that these concepts were too narrow, and had to be replaced by the notion of 'utterance', being the actual representation of a speaking person's use of language in a concrete setting (such as 'speech acting'). To use another terminology, the usual concentration on 'minimal' units of expression is too restrictive, both from the point of view of extension (it comprises too little) and of that of intension (it just hasn't enough substance, or the substance has the wrong make-up). To clarify this, let me spend a few lines on the so-called 'crisis' of micropragmatics, such as it became apparent in the development of the theory of speech acts after Grice (the 'neo-Gricean paradigm', as it is often called).

4.2. Micropragmatics in crisis: the Neo-Griceans and their problems.
Grice and his original followers agreed that, in order to be not just correct, but efficient, a speech act had to obey certain conditions. Some of these had been formulated by Searle (and earlier by Austin, the latter having put his conditions in a rather loose fashion, compared to Searle's somewhat pinching philosophical straitjacket). Grice's Cooperative Principle and the attending four maxims are well-known to most and will not be commented upon here; what I want to show is that many people realized that there was something strange about having to define efficient cooperative behavior, using abstract philosophical qualities such as quantity, quality, relation, and manner. The principle and its maxims worked all right for many cases; but there was some doubt about whether they were always and equally necessary. Vice versa, could one think of other, either more extended or more restricted formulations of successful cooperative behavior? This is where the Neo-Griceans (a collective term for all those who work in some Grice-inspired pattern of explanation) come into our field of vision.

Among the Neo-Griceans, the most famous became Sperber and Wilson, who in their 1986 (1995) book *Relevance* argue that we in reality don't need all those maxims, but that one single principle, that of relevance (cf. Grice's relation maxim) should be sufficient and necessary to account for people's communicative and cognitive behavior. Sperber and Wilson assume that in every communication, the participants aim for optimal relevance (1986; 144, 155); however, what this relevance is, and how it is defined, remains unclear: relevance itself remains an axiomatic, context-free principle. Despite its resounding success (especially in the British linguistic environment), the theory has been attacked on various counts.

Here, without going into details of purely technical interest, I merely want to make the point that Sperber and Wilson's theory, just as its predecessors, is defective in that it takes its point of departure in isolated, mostly speaker-originated utterances. (Occasionally, when deemed useful, these utterances are expanded into mini-dialogues between some imagined interlocutors, not much different from Saussure's 'talking heads').

The most important question to be asked in this, as in other Neo-Gricean theorizing, is by now a familiar one, viz.: How can we know what is relevant in an utterance? Or: What makes an utterance relevant? This question is parallel to the one asked in the 'classical' speech act paradigm, namely: What force does an utterance have, and how can we be sure it works in the desired fashion?

One cannot deny that this question has a certain interest. But the interest is limited to the cases where input and successful output seem to stand in a clearly visible relationship to one another. But what about the cases where this relation does not apply? This is where the so-called 'indirect speech act problem' raises its ugly head.

4.3. The indirect speech act problem.

The problem is briefly this:

Given that we have pre-established, 'canonical' expressions for performing certain kinds of linguistic activity (such as a verb 'to promise' for the speech act of promising; the grammatical mood of imperative for executing an order; and so on), why is it then that people, when promising, ordering, etc. often, nay usually, prefer to choose a form of the language that only indirectly relates to the act to be performed? For instance, if I want to know the time of day, I don't phrase my query as a simple question ('What time is it?') but as a request for information as to the ability of the addressee to tell me the time of day ('Can you tell me the time (, please)?').[4]

The point to note here is that it is not the speech act as such that performs an action. What linguists and philosophers have called the (perlocutionary) 'effect' of a speech act is, in the last instance, dependent on the situation in which the act is performed. Given the right situation, the actual wording that I can use in order to obtain a particular effect may vary enormously (think of the innumerable ways in which one can ask people to close the door: from 'It's cold in here' to 'I'm allergic to draughts' or 'My grandmother always told me that a door should be either open or closed', and so

---

[4] Some of these indirect acts have become so ingrained and almost standardized that we don't perceive them as indirect any longer: the indirect speech act of asking somebody to sit down ('Won't you have a seat') has completely replaced the direct order form ('Sit down'), normally only used in formal contexts, such as the courthouse, or to dogs and the like.

on ad infinitum). Conversely, even the most perfectly executed speech act, when uttered in the wrong situation, will fail to have its effect (recall Stephen Levinson's example where he goes up in the middle of the night with a bottle of champagne to the ship to be christened the next morning, and pronounces the words: 'I hereby name this good ship the Stephen C. Levinson', while ruining a perfectly good bottle of champagne to absolutely no purpose; cf. Levinson 1983; 229, slightly modified).

Hence, for a speech act to be successful, the first condition is that it be performed according to the situational circumstances that are in force. This insight is of course not altogether new: it was formulated as early in 1972 by Dell Hymes in his well-known article on 'speech events', and then again by Levinson in a less-well known (but recently reprinted) article on 'types of activity' (1979. Briefly, what these viewpoints have in common with mine is that the acts we perform, are conditioned by the 'affordances' of the situation, as I have called it elsewhere, appropriating a term originally due to the psychologist James J. Gibson (1979; Mey 2001; 220-221). All speech acts (and not only the indirect ones) are in essence situated acts; that is to say that their success depends on how well their executors are able to adjust themselves to the necessities of the situation. The act takes precedence over the word; but the situation takes precedence over the act. (Basically, that is what my theory of 'pragmatic acts' is all about; see the relevant chapter 8 in Mey 2001).

4.4. Macropragmatics: from the outside in.
For speech act theorists, the problem of the indirect speech act is like the canary in the miners' cage: it alerts us to the existence of unknown dangers and problems. The danger, in our case, is the excessive reliance on the linguistic shape of the act rather than on its situational conditions (undoubtedly a taint or a legacy from the blind reliance on the criterion of 'correctness' in contemporary syntactic studies). Such a reliance may make us close our eyes to what is really going on; clearly, then, we must remove the blindfold and re-orient ourselves to the *situation*.

The role of the situation can aptly be described by using the metaphor of motion that I employed earlier: while classical speech act theory starts from the speaker's words, and traces their trajectory all the way to a hopefully successful situation, the pragmatic view starts with the situation, and tries to find the successful linguistic (and other) elements that correspond to the desired act and its performance. While the former motion is centrifugal, the later is centripetal.[5] The description of the situational speech act (or 'speech event') replaces the individual speech act as the unit of description.

---

[5] My use of these notions should not be confused with that of similar concepts by Bakhtin, especially in his work 'Discourse in the novel'; see Morson & Emerson (1990; 139-140).

The descriptive emphasis is thus no longer on describing individual speech acts (as it was for Searle and his followers). What the speech event does is understandable only in terms of the language used; conversely, the individual speech acts make sense only in the event. More recently, this view has gained considerable support among anthropologists and linguists; thus, Hanks states that "meaning arises out of the interaction between language and circumstances, rather than being encapsulated in the language itself" (1996; 266), that is to say, rather than being encoded in units of meaning and administered by way of syntactic rules.[6]

5. Conclusion: Where do we go from here?

We have seen how the traditional paradigm of language study and analysis has undergone drastic changes in the course of the last century. From being a strictly structurally oriented paradigm (itself replacing the earlier, classical philological one), it has become a pragmatic one, in the sense that the focus of interest no longer is on the rules of a grammar, but on the ways that the users do things with their words in communication and activity.

We have further seen how the initial impact for this paradigm change came not from linguistics but from the philosophers of language. However, the latter, too, got stuck in the (implicitly recognized) communicative model of the linguistic tradition (the 'talking heads'), which was based on a double fallacy: it failed to recognize the communicative person as a whole, and it tried to explain the phenomena of language 'from the inside out', 'centrifugally', that is, starting from the speaker (or better, the speaker's head). This *micropragmatic* approach was then gradually complemented by a *macropragmatic* view, in which the questions to be raised were asked 'centripetally', that is to say, starting from the world and the entire context of communication, zooming in on the individual speaker(s) as representative(s) of a societal conglomeration (or 'class', in the parlance of Marxism).

The wisdom to retain from the micropragmatic approach is this: when communicating, what you don't say may be as important, or even more important, than what you do say. The Gricean implicatures are a prime example of this tendency. The macropragmatic approach adds to this the observation that we only can say what we are empowered by society to say, i.e. by our 'affordances', as I have called them. These affordances have to do not only with what is in the mind, but to a great degree also with what the mind *and body* can transmit; thus, when analyzing conversation, it should be a minimum demand on methodology that one incorporates the body's role (posture, gaze, facial expressions, breath, and so on): the body

---

[6] See Enfield (1998) for an enlightening discussion of this issue.

does not just accompany speech, but is an essential part of the total communicative act.

But what can these changes tell us in relation to the theme of our conference: 'Changing Philologies'?

First of all, it is not just philology that is changing. Rather, what we see is a wholly new orientation of the linguistic and language study paradigm, including of course the philologies and the way we put them to use, e.g. in a teaching situation.

Second, as to the changes that actually have taken place during the last century, I am thinking of the successful paradigms of Conversational Analysis, of studies on the linguistic and cognitive aspects of machine-human interaction, as studied in the new discipline of Cognitive Technology (Gorayska & Mey 1996), of studies in the pragmatic-semantic interface (Turner & Jaszczolt 1996ff), of pragmatically oriented studies of linguistic interaction in institutions such as the schools, the psychiatric interview, the courtrooms, the hospital, and so on (e.g. Heller & Martin-Jones 2001, Caffi 2000, Magalhães 2000), of anthropologically oriented pragmatic studies on communication (e.g. Hanks 1996), of Neo-Gricean studies on problems of negation, relevance, mitigation, anaphora, and implicature (e.g. Horn 1989, Green 1989, Blakemore 1992, Huang 2000, Levinson 2000), and so on and so forth – not to forget the proliferation of textbooks and general treatises on pragmatics, as exemplified in the classical works by Gazdar (1979), Leech (1983), Levinson(1983), supplemented by later-comers such as Mey (1993, 2001), Marmaridou (1995, 2000), Thomas (1996), Grundy (1996), Verschueren (1999), and others.

Third, while all these authors somehow or other support the paradigm change, there is one aspect of pragmatics that I think is of extreme practical importance when it comes to changing our views on philology in the 'classical' sense (as exemplified by the quote from Wilamowitz-Moellendorf that I gave you in the beginning of this talk). A living culture can only be transmitted and expanded in a pragmatic way. That is, we cannot just study texts; we must reproduce the life of the people behind the texts: "it is the task of philology to rekindle this life of the past through science", as the great German philologist admonishes us, and this holds not only of texts of the past, but for those of the present as well.

Fourth, this point of view has grave implications for the way we see our tasks as e.g. teachers of language and culture. Earlier (in fact, during the latter two-thirds of the last century), grammar-based approaches had been typically disfavored, the standard model of foreign language teaching, in French called 'thème et version' being gradually replaced by an approach that went under the name of 'communication-oriented teaching'. It was not always clear what one meant by 'communication', and in particular, what was to be communicative in this approach. Often, it concentrated on generating some rough and ready 'competence' in situations of everyday life, so that the young learner could manage on his or her own in a situation with foreign language speakers, either at home or in the foreign country, without too much emphasis on grammar rules or correctness of expression. For some time, it looked indeed as if this trend was going to carry the day, over the more or less dead bodies of a great number of old-fashioned language teachers who deplored the downfall of grammar and with that, the elimination of the ability to express oneself more or less adequately on subjects of interest that went beyond the daily sphere of shopping and making acquaintances in bars.

Fifth and finally, the above considerations have led me to formulate the paradox of what is often called 'pragmatic competence' (as distinguished from, and complementing, linguistic and/or communicative competence), as follows.

Being pragmatically competent means that you are able to exploit the non-explicit components of a communicative situation: e.g. what one is allowed to bring up as a subject of conversation with strangers; what one can safely say when questioned by a police office or by a judge in court (here, the Gricean maxim of quantity is often of extreme importance!); what kind of body language should accompany a request for a favor (a very important part of Japanese communicative style); what register should one use when addressing different classes of people: students, colleagues, domestic partners, children, and so on) – all these situations carry with them a component that cannot be described in simple rules of grammar or behavior.

Now here is the paradox: you may have been told that linguistic, especially grammatical, competence is not to be considered as essential in order to communicate. But the pragmatics of the situation will tell you that what is not said, may be more important than what is actually said. In other words, even if you may not need to know all the linguistic rules to make a successful application; your application will be the more successful, the better you manage those linguistic and other rules. (Think of that old, very non-PC joke: If you are from Manchester or Liverpool, and are having a job interview in London, take a course in sign language).

Summing up, the changing philologies of the 20th century seem to have reverted to their origin: philology as the study of the entire human being. Simultaneously, the study of language (including grammar) has come full circle to where it rejoins that of communication (including conversational interaction). Pragmatically speaking, we consider non-linguistic communicative competencies to be equally important as the linguistic ones. But in reaction to certain tendencies in the 'communicative competence' program, we will not discredit the power that resides in the appropriate use of language, inasmuch as it reflects the affordances that our society offers its members at any given moment, in any given situation. In this sense, philology is an integral part of pragmatics, and should be given its proper place and stature in a future vision of language studies, both theoretical and practical.

References

Benne, Christian: 2001. 'Zwischen Germanistik und 'Tysk' oder Gegenwart und Zukunft des Deutschstudiums in Dänemark. Fünf Thesen'. In: *Das ästhetische Wiesel*, Heft 3. Odense, University of Southern Denmark.

Bakhtin, Mikhail M.: 1994. 'The problem of speech genres'. In: Michael Holquist & Caryl Emerson, eds., *Speech genres and other late essays* (translated by Vern McGee). Austin, University of Texas Press. pp. 60-102. [1979]

Blakemore, Diane: 1992. *Understanding utterances*. Oxford, Blackwell.

Bloomfield, Leonard: 1950. *Language*. London, George Allen & Unwin. [1933]

Caffi, Claudia: 2000. *La mitigazione. Un approccio pragmatico alla comunicazione nei contesti terapeutici*. Pavia, Cooperativa Libraria Universitaria and Münster: LIT.

Dostoevskij, Fedor M: 1965. Zapiski iz podpol'ja [Notes from Underground]. Letchworth, Herts, Bradda Books. [1864]

Enfield, Nick: 1998. 'On the indispensability of semantics: Defining the "vacuous".' In: E Pluribus Una: *A Festschrift for Anna Wierzbicka*. Odense, Odense University Press. pp. 285-304.

Gazdar, Gerald: 1979. *Pragmatics: Implicature, presupposition, and logical form*. New York & San Francisco, Academic Press.

Gorayska, Barbara & Jacob L. Mey, eds: 1996. *Cognitive Technology: In search of a humane interface*. Amsterdam & Oxford, Elsevier North Holland.

Gibson, James J.: 1979. *The ecological approach to visual perception*. Boston, Mass., Houghton Mifflin.

Green, Georgia N.: 1989. *Pragmaticas and natural language*. Hillsdale, N.J., Erlbaum.

Grice, H. Paul: 1975. 'Logic and conversation'. In: Peter Cole, ed.: *Syntax and Semantics*, vol 9. New York, Academic Press. pp. 41-58.

Grundy, Peter: 1996. *Doing pragmatics*. London, Edward Arnold.

Gumperz, John J. & Dell Hymes, eds.: 1972. *Directions in sociolinguistics: The ethnography of communication*. Oxford, Basil Blackwell.

Gumperz, John J. and Stephen C. Levinson, eds.: 1996. *Rethinking linguistic relativity*. Cambridge, Cambridge University Press.

Hanks, William F.: 1996. *Language and communicative practices*. Boulder, Col., Westview Press.

Heller, Monica & Marilyn Martin-Jones: 2001. *Voices of authority*. Oxford & Boston, Blackwell.

Hjelmslev, Louis: 1943. *Omkring sprogteoriens grundlæggelse*. København, Munksgaard. (Translated as: *Prolegomena to a theory of language* by Francis Whitfield. Bloomington, Ind., University of Indiana Press. 1953)

Horn, Lawrence: 1989. *A natural history of negation*. Chicago, University of Chicago Press.

Huang, Yan: 2000. *Anaphora: A cross-linguistic study*. Oxford, Oxford University Press.

Hymes, Dell: 1972. 'Models of the interaction of language and social life'. In: Gumperz and Hymes, eds. pp. 35-71.

Leech, Geoffrey: 1983. *Principles of pragmatics*. London, Longman.

Levinson, Stephen C.: 1979. 'Activity types and language'. *Linguistics* 17(5/6); pp. 365-399. (Reprinted 1992 in P. Drew & J. Heritage, eds.: 'Talk at Work': *Interaction in institutional settings*. Cambridge, Cambridge University Press; pp. 66-100).

Levinson, Stephen C: 1983. *Pragmatics*. Cambridge, Cambridge University Press.

Levinson, Stephen C.: 2000. *Presumptive Meanings: The theory of generalized conversational implicature*. Cambridge, Mass., MIT Press.

Magalhães, Izabel M.: 2000. *Eu e tu: A constituição do sujeito no discurso médico*. Brasília, D.F., Thesaurus Editora.

Marmaridou, A. Sophia S.: 1995. *Cognitive and social aspects of pragmatic meaning: A contribution to experiental realism*. Athens, Parousia.

Marmaridou, A. Sophia S.: 2000. *Pragmatic meaning and cognition*. Amsterdam & Philadelphia, John Benjamins.

Marx, Karl & Friedrich Engels: 1974. *Die deutsche Ideologie*. Berlin, Dietz. (MEW Band 3) [1848].

Mey, Jacob L.: 1985. *Whose language? A study in linguistic pragmatics*. Amsterdam & Philadelphia, John Benjamins.

Mey, Jacob L.: 2001. *Pragmatics: An introduction*. Oxford & Boston, Blackwell. (Second enlarged and revised edition) [1993].

Morson, Gary S. & Caryl Emerson: 1990. *Mikhail Bakhtin: Creation of a Prosaics*. Stanford, Calif., Stanford University Press.

Saussure, Ferdinand de: 1949. *Cours de linguistique générale*. Paris, Payot. [1916]

Searle, John R.: 1969. *Speech acts: An essay in the philosophy of language*. Cambridge, Cambridge University Press.

Sperber, Dan & Deirdre Wilson: 1995. *Relevance: Communication and cognition*. Oxford, Blackwell. [1986].

Thomas, Jenny: 1996. *Meaning in interaction: An introduction to pragmatics*. London, Longman.

Turner, Ken P. & Katarzyna Jaszczolt, eds.: 1996ff. *CRISPI: Current research in the pragmatic-semantics interface*. Oxford, Elsevier Science.

Verschueren, Jef: 1999. *Understanding pragmatics*. London, Edward Arnold.

Wilamowitz-Moellendorf, Ulrich von: 1998. *Geschichte der Philologie*. Leipzig, Teubner. [1921]

Complex Implied Form, Leisure Pursuits, and Cultural Studies

by

Nigel Fabb

University of Strathclyde, Glasgow

Introduction

Leisure pursuits are among the cultural practices which a cultural studies might examine. It is common to see leisure pursuits as meeting some more general human need, perhaps the need to experience and engage in the 'ludic' (Huizinga 1938); these experiences of leisure relate to aesthetic experience and like aesthetic experience can be understood at least sometimes as complex. In this paper I ask whether the study of leisure pursuits can be integrated into a more general cultural studies by specifically exploring the complexities of both their form and their content, and I will pursue an approach to this based on linguistic pragmatics.

In this paper I begin by looking at form and content in literary texts, and suggest an integrated approach to complexity in form and content, based on linguistic pragmatics; in this I draw on current work published as Fabb (2002a,b). The second part of the paper is more speculative, and extends the account of literary form and literary content to everyday leisure pursuits such as birdwatching, going to the seaside, and so on.

How does form hold?

Before looking at complexity in content I want to ask what I think is a difficult question about form, which is this:

How does form hold – of a text, or of an object, or of a practice?

I suggest that there are two answers to this question, because there are two kinds of form which are so different from one another that it is almost misleading to give them similar names. I focus in this section on the two kinds of form which hold specifically of a literary text.

The first kind of form is exemplified by syntactic or phonological form in language. These kinds of form are constitutive: phonological form is what enables a speech sound to exist, and a word must belong to a word class (such as 'noun') in order for it to be part of a sentence. The constitutive nature of these kinds of form means that they are also determinate: a text has a specific linguistic form (putting aside structural ambiguity), which can in principle be discovered. While it is possible to produce utterances and written texts which are not made of linguistic form[1], linguistic form is the basis of everyday speech and writing and thus should hold with a very high degree of consistency of everyday speech and writing. Constitutive form is ontologically expensive: we make a significant ontological commitment by claiming that it exists. Linguistic Theory has offered us good evidence that phonological and syntactic form exist. We might ask whether any of the kinds of form which we find in literary texts are constitutive form of this kind, bearing in mind the ontological expense of positing such form. I suggest that metrical form is this kind of form. Thus a certain description holds true of the vast majority of lines in the meter 'iambic pentameter' in English. This description is as follows:

The iambic pentameter line must have ten projected[2] syllables.

Given these ten syllables, a stressed syllable in a polysyllabic word can only appear in position 1,2,4,6,8 or 10 in an iambic pentameter line.

This describes a constitutive form which we could call 'constitutive form of iambic pentameter', and there is a very high likelihood that any line in iambic pentameter will have exactly this form. It is the reliability of this claim which makes it plausible that this is a kind of constitutive form, like phonological or syntactic form.

Note however that this does not describe all aspects of what we might generally call 'iambic pentameter'; in iambic pentameter lines there is a tendency for the line to fit a pattern of alternating unstressed and stressed syllables, many of which are monosyllables and thus do not fall under the formal description made earlier. This tendency represents a fundamentally different kind of form, which is tendential or approximative rather than

---

[1] Such as imitations of natural sounds. It is also possible to imitate linguistic form – and texts like *Finnegans Wake* do precisely this; they are not made from linguistic form but they imitate texts which are made from linguistic form.

[2] As has been known in English metrical theory since the sixteenth century, not every syllable counts in scanning a line of poetry; the syllables which can be excluded can be simply defined, on phonological or positional grounds (eg. a vowel preceding another vowel may not be counted; a final unstressed syllable is not counted).

determinate. I suggest that this aspect of iambic pentameter form is not a kind of constitutive form (which is always fully present or determinate rather than approximate), but is something quite different, a kind of implied form. Thus the description below might be called 'implied form of iambic pentameter', in contrast to the constitutive form of iambic pentameter:

> The rhythm of the line approximates to a pattern x / x / x / x / x /.
>
> If the rhythm of a line is x / x / x / x / x / then the line is in iambic pentameter.

Most kinds of literary form are kinds of implied form. While the study of constitutive form is analogous to the study of phonology or syntax, the study of implied form falls under the purview of pragmatics. I now briefly explain how form might be implied.

The study of implicature is the study of propositions which are warranted by evidence provided by the utterance/text, in the context of what the interpreter knows. For the most part, the propositions which are studied in pragmatics are propositions about some reality external to the text. But propositions can also be about the text itself. Thus a sonnet might communicate the implicature 'I am in love with a certain woman' which is a representation of some external reality, and at the same time might communicate the implicature 'This text is a sonnet' which is a representation of the text itself. The latter kind of implicature is an implicature about form, which is to say that it is an instance of implied form. I suggest that the tendency for iambic pentameter lines to approximate to a certain rhythmic pattern can be understood as the text warranting the implicature 'this line is in iambic pentameter'. Thus the form 'iambic pentameter' can hold of a text in two fundamentally different ways; it can hold as a kind of constitutive form (a certain number of projected syllables, the polysyllables placed specifically) and at the same time as a kind of implied form (the text tells us that it is in iambic pentameter by approximating to a rhythmic pattern).

Any theory of linguistic pragmatics should be able to give us a way of understanding how form is implied. This is because 'implied form' is just the name for a certain set of contents of propositions (propositions which are about the text). However, I believe there are some advantages in choosing Relevance Theory (Sperber and Wilson 1995), which is simple and ontologically parsimonious, and offers us some powerful tools – the notion of strength, the notion of explicature – along with its established theoretical practice of applying these notions to literary and cultural material. In Relevance Theory, most implicature works by the logical rule of modus ponens, which has the form: 'A, if A then B, therefore B'.

> This text has fourteen lines of iambic pentameter.

If this text has fourteen lines of iambic pentameter then it is a sonnet.
-----therefore----
This text is a sonnet.

Deductions of this kind can be used to explain most aspects of how a formal aspect of a text is able to imply other formal aspects. Sperber and Wilson suggest that propositions hold with degrees of strength, and that the strength of premises affects the strength of the conclusions. In this case, the 'if..then' clause is slightly weak (we know that not all texts in fourteen lines of iambic pentameter are sonnets), and so the conclusion 'This text is a sonnet' is correspondingly weakened. Modus ponens can explain how one kind of form leads to the inference of another. We need another mechanism to understand how this process starts, how the text sets off the inferential process. For most kinds of meaning, the content of implicatures is derived from an utterance or text by developing a logical form from the text, and then by an inferential process filling in any gaps in the logical form to produce a full proposition, which is an explicature. I suggest we take an analogous view of the development of propositions about form; an explicature such as 'this text has fourteen lines' or 'this text has the rhythm x / x / x / x / x /' can be inferred directly from the text as what we might call a formal explicature. We can use this as a way of understanding how form can be approximative, by exploiting Sperber and Wilson's notion of interpretive resemblance. They argue that another implicative strategy, in addition to modus ponens, is for one proposition to imply another because it resembles it. This enables us to understand how form can be approximative. If the text actually has a rhythm x / x / x x x / x / then it resembles and hence implies the rhythm x / x / x / x / x /. In fact, strictly speaking a text with the rhythm x / x / x x x / x / implies – somewhat weakly – the proposition:

The rhythm of the line is x / x / x / x / x /.

Thus we can understand approximation as resemblance, where one form resembles another and thus implies it.

These are the mechanisms by which form can be implied – the development of formal explicatures, the use of interpretive resemblance in some cases, and the use of modus ponens. In principle any kind of form can be implied in this way, and in the absence of evidence to the contrary I suggest we assume that literary form is generally implied in this way. This kind of form is ontologically cheap; we are making no ontological claims when we allow the term 'sonnet' into an implicature – it is just part of a proposition, and we do not have to have some notion of the Ideal Sonnet to which actual texts approximate. When we consider literary form, we can distinguish three general kinds of form: pattern relative to a template (eg. meter), division into parts (eg. into lines, stanzas, narrative episodes), and genre. I have shown how pattern can be implied (while allowing also that some aspects of pattern might be constitutive). Division into parts is not quite so obviously implied, because it superficially resembles syntactic form which is a kind of constitutive form. But while there is often a loose relation between linguistic form and the divisions of literary texts (eg. lines often loosely correspond to sentences), it is the looseness of the relation which gives the game away. Good evidence for this comes from a practice which is demonstrated in Fabb (2002a), which is to take a text with variable line length – here, Matthew Arnold's 'Dover Beach' (1867) – and lay it out as prose, and then try to reverse-engineer the text into verse. This is what the delineated layout looks like. The reader may wish to try reconstructing the presence of line boundaries.

> The sea is calm to-night. The tide is full, the moon lies fair upon the Straits; on the French coast, the light gleams, and is gone; the cliffs of England stand, glimmering and vast, out in the tranquil bay. Come to the window, sweet is the night air! Only, from the long line of spray where the ebb meets the moon-blanched sand, listen! you hear the grating roar of pebbles which the waves suck back, and fling, at their return, up the high strand, begin, and cease, and then again begin, with tremulous cadence slow, and bring the eternal note of sadness in. Sophocles long ago heard it on the Aegæan, and it brought into his mind the turbid ebb and flow of human misery; we find also in the sound a thought, hearing it by this distant northern sea. The sea of faith was once, too, at the full, and round earth's shore lay like the folds of a bright girdle furled; but now I only hear its melancholy, long, withdrawing roar, retreating to the breath of the night-wind down the vast edges drear and naked shingles of the world. Ah, love, let us be true to one another! For the world, which seems to lie before us like a land of dreams, so various, so beautiful, so new, hath really neither joy, nor love, nor light, nor certitude, nor peace, nor help for pain; and we are here as on a darkling plain swept with confused alarms of struggle and flight, where ignorant armies clash by night.

For this and similar kinds of text there are two interesting results; the first is that it is difficult to find the line boundaries, and the second is that people draw on evidence from the text and their literary knowledge (ie. a stock of 'if..then' propositions, as part of modus ponens based inferences) as a way of reconstructing the text. Most people try to rewrite 'Dover Beach' as iambic pentameter (unrhymed, and hence as blank verse) and indeed the text seems to justify this interpretation. In fact Arnold laid it out in variable-length iambic lines with rhyme, not as iambic pentameter. This exercise suggests that the printed lineation of 'Dover Beach' in fact competes with various other possible lineations which are immanent in the text. Thus we can see lineation as implied rather than constitutive; we take elements of the text (such as layout, but also rhyme, meter, parallelism, pausing) as evidence for its division into parts. Finally, the possibility that genre is implied rather than (as Aristotle would have held) constitutive fits well with the indeterminacy of genre, genre mixing, genre emergence and so on. 'Dover Beach' is in fact somewhat ambiguous generically; to some extent it implies that it is an ode (by its heterometricality), while its final nine lines appear to be an emergent sonnet, ending on a couplet.

Sperber and Wilson remind us that communication takes place at a risk; there is no guarantee that any implicature is true of the text (in the sense that it was intended by its author). Rather than holding absolutely, implicatures carry a certain degree of strength which corresponds to the certainty with which they are held to arise from the text. This means that implicatures are in principle capable of being vague and indeterminate, and it also means that a single text can give rise to incompatible implicatures which in relation to each other are ambiguous or contradictory. If we see most kinds of form as implied, then this means that most kinds of form are also capable of holding strongly or weakly, and can be vague and indeterminate, and can be ambiguous or contradictory. This has characteristically been argued in literary theory, and we now have an explanation for it drawn from linguistic pragmatics. I suggest that these potential characteristics of form are kinds of complexity, and that these kinds of complexity are experienced as aesthetic.

This approach to form means that form can be emergent. Many texts have a form which has been seen before in other texts and thus the experienced reader will already have knowledge of these kinds of form expressed as 'if...then' propositions ('if this text is a sonnet then it will have fourteen lines'). But the reader might equally develop new propositions, describing form in ways not previously described. In Milton's *Paradise Lost* the first two lines begin with the word 'of' which might allow the reader to invent a weak hypothesis along the lines of: 'if this word is 'of' then it is at the beginning of a line'. Statistically, 'of' is more likely to appear at the beginning of the line (28% of all instances of 'of') than anywhere else in *Paradise Lost*, so this proposition might be taken as a kind of emergent form. Interestingly, it holds well for many post-Miltonic texts; for example in Wordsworth's 'Tintern Abbey' twenty-three of the sixty instances of 'of' are line-initial (Fabb 2000b). This is a kind of form which is emergent, and in fact holds rather weakly; perhaps it gives 'Tintern Abbey' a kind of weak aura of Miltonic style. Emergence is what we would expect for implied form because implied form is ontologically cheap and any new kind of implied form fundamentally a matter of just formulating a new proposition; in contrast, we would expect emergence much more rarely for constitutive form. A good comparison is the invention of new nouns (easy, because it involves a new kind of content) compared to the invention of new grammatical words (hard, because it involves a new kind of constitutive form).

In summary, I have argued that while there are limited kinds of constitutive literary form, most kinds of literary form are implied form. This gives literary form the potential to be complex (vague, indeterminate, ambiguous, contradictory) and to be emergent. In the next part of this paper I will briefly discuss some ways in which literary contents can have similar characteristics, and I will then speculate on the relation between these characteristics and aesthetic experience.

Complex contents and aesthetic experience
In the previous section I suggested that most kinds of literary form are implied form. This means that most kinds of literary form are actually best understood as kinds of content: the content of propositions about the text which are warranted by the text, such as 'this text is in iambic pentameter' or 'this text is a sonnet'. I further suggested that implied form benefits aesthetically from the potential complexities of being a kind of content. In this section I briefly consider some of the aesthetic benefits of complexity of referential content.

'Dover Beach' is complex in form because it implies multiple and incompatible possible lineations and multiple genres. These are characteristic kinds of complexity; at the same time 'Dover Beach' is also characteristically complex in meaning, in ways associated with the tradition of the sublime. In Kant's account, the experience of the sublime is an experience of epistemological contradiction (Kant 1952[1790]; 90-91).

> ... the sublime is to be found in an object even devoid of form, so far as it immediately involves, or else by its presence provokes, a representation of limitnessness, yet with a super-added thought of its totality.

In its manifestations, as Wordsworth's 'spots of time', Woolf's 'moments of being', Joyce's 'epiphanies', Brecht's 'Gestus', Benjamin's 'Jetztzeit', Barthes's 'punctum', and so on, the special moment of the sublime is often derived from a specific kind of contradictory experience. Thus Wordsworth on Snowdon experiences the sublime when he sees the mountains in the clouds simultaneously as islands in the sea: *both-and instead of either-or*, as the architect Robert Venturi puts it (Venturi 1977). What is interesting about these contradictions is that they become somewhat stereotyped; there are certain typical places in which they occur, certain typical kinds of contradiction. In 'Dover Beach' there are two characteristic kinds of contradiction. The first is the presence of liminal zones, places which are nothing other than the boundary between two other places, and thus – I suggest – inherently contradictory in the sense that being in a liminal zone is being nowhere. The liminal zones in 'Dover

Beach' are the beach itself, between land and sea, and the window at which the poet stands ('Come to the window...'), between inside and outside, culture and nature. These specific liminal zones, along with doorways, stairs, the horizon, and so on, are very characteristic places for the experience of the sublime in Romanticism and Modernism. The other characteristically Romantic/Modernist mode of contradiction seen in this text is the experience of being an individual amidst a crowd, which suddenly emerges at the end of the poem. Here the contradictions are specifically the individual against the mass and are part of a set of contradictions pitting the small against the big and the articulate against the dense.

Thus 'Dover Beach' illustrates two characteristic complexities of content. One kind of complexity involves location: being between two places, hence *both-and instead of either-or*. The other kind of complexity involves the experience of opposition, such as being an individual in a crowd. It is possible that Arnold's combination of these specific kinds of sublimity is a nod in the direction of the example in Longinus (Dorsch 1965; 133): 'straightaway a countless host ranged along the beaches and sent out a cry "Tunny!".' I suggest that both kinds of complexity are best seen as arising at the level of implicature. Thus 'being a liminal zone' is a description holding of a represented place, but holding to a certain extent rather than absolutely. Beaches are liminal zones in some respects (as the boundary between land and sea) but are not inherently or constitutively liminal; the beach is 'nowhere' in some regards (eg. if it is seen as the boundary between two major opposed zones, the land and the sea) but it is also 'somewhere' (eg. if you are building sandcastles on it). Nevertheless, beaches clearly have a greater potential to be liminal than some other places, and perhaps this is why beaches turn up with some frequency as places where the sublime is experienced. The same can be said of contradictions such as 'being an individual in a crowd', where there is certainly potential for inferring this as a contradiction, but where such inferences can be strengthened or weakened by other thoughts about the situation. The characteristic mode of the sublime in literature is to take a situation or location which has the potential for contradiction, and to point up and develop exactly this potential for contradiction. Thus for example the Wordsworthian notion that recollection and retelling are greater than the original experience itself suggest both that poetry develops a possibility which is only a potential in the original experience, and that cognitive – inferential – work on the situation or location is an essential part of the experience of the sublime. While the sublime characteristically strikes suddenly, it is also experienced as a full and complex cognitive experience.

In the previous few paragraphs I have suggested that there are similarities between the experience of complex form and the experience of complex content. I suggested that one of the ways in which literary texts deliver aesthetic experience to us is by presenting us with opportunities both in form and in content to develop inferences which lead us into contradiction and ambiguity, vagueness and indeterminacy. In the next section of this paper I consider whether leisure activities have the potential to do something similar, and hence that we might be able to develop a poetics of leisure as part of a larger agenda for cultural studies.

The poetics of leisure

There are two primary disciplinary modes of cultural studies, at least in the United Kingdom. One is a development of the textually-oriented modes of British linguistics, and involves textual analysis, critical linguistics, and stylistics. The other involves the applications and goals of disciplines such as sociology, ethnography, and anthropology. Both of these modes in principle allow for a poetics of leisure which would look specifically at the ways in which the forms and contents and performances of leisure pursuits are experienced as pleasurable and aesthetically significant. Thus the linguistic side of cultural studies can draw on stylistics and the sociological side of cultural studies can draw on ethnopoetics. A poetics of leisure is a legitimate application of either or both of these two general disciplinary components of cultural studies.

Various kinds of poetics of leisure can be imagined. We might for example follow Bauman (1975) and focus on performance (see also Bauman and Briggs 1990). Bauman develops Jakobson's (1960) idea that the poetic function is achieved by a focus on the message, that is, by the use of ostensive form, form which is noticed by the users of the text. Bauman suggests that form is ostensive in poetic practice because poetic practice is a performance which asks to be evaluated, and adherence to formal conventions offers a yardstick for evaluation. Following Bauman, we would look at the extent to which leisure activities are performed for an audience, and the extent to which they demand evaluation, and whether that evaluation is in terms of adherence to rules. The fact that many leisure activities involve societies and competitions of various kinds, and ostensive displays (of equipment, clothing, artefacts, etc.) would fit with the possibility that leisure activities are performed.

Another way in which we might explore a poetics of leisure, overlapping with Bauman's focus on performance and evaulation, but from a different angle, is to ask whether leisure activities have the same kinds of complexity in form and content which we have seen in poetry. Leisure activities might thus offer the same cognitive rewards, through complexity and contradiction, as those offered by poetry. For Lévi-Strauss, culture is in part made from a set of structures and oppositions, such as the binary opposition of 'raw' and 'cooked' and its neutralization in 'rotten'. It is these which make cultural practices and objects 'good to think'. Sperber (1975) argues that one of the things which makes a cultural practice – such as a symbolism – 'good to think' is when the cultural practice does not quite make sense. Thus a thought which contains an indeterminate term, hence a schematic proposition rather than a fully specified one, can be a rich source of speculation and inference, and its indeterminacy also appears often to be associated with strong propositional attitudes; our deepest beliefs may also be our least paraphraseable beliefs. Sperber's twin notions, that we get inferential complexity from cultural practices and objects and that this complexity has experiential consequences, are the basis for my earlier speculations about literary practice and complexities of form and content. I now return to Sperber's original anthroplogical concerns, cultural practices in general and not just officially aesthetic practices, to ask whether we can build a project from the notion that complexity can be one of the bases for the attractions of leisure activities, and hence makes these activities 'good to think'.

Ways of exploring complexity in leisure pursuits

In this final part of the paper I propose some strategies for exploring complexity in form and content of leisure pursuits which are not classified as kinds of art.

Most leisure activities are densely commented, annotated and represented in handbooks, guidebooks and magazines; these are amongst the best selling publications. One mode in cultural studies is to examine the leisure activities by analyzing these texts, as though these texts tell us what people do when they engage in these leisure activities. An alternative is to see the buying, possessing, displaying, carrying around, and reading of these books as integral parts of the leisure activities. This has various advantages. First, we can understand the books not as representing the leisure activities, but as a way of dreaming or symbolizing the leisure activities; cookbooks tell the amateur cook what to do, but they are also an imaginary version of what food, cooking and eating are. Jameson (1981) argues that nineteenth century novels are the dreams of nineteenth century society, the political unconscious resolving its contradictions in the dreamwork; similarly we might see representations of leisure activities not fundamentally as realistic representations but as fantasies. As fantasies they are capable themselves of being contradictory, but more interestingly they have the potential to be contradictory relative to the cultural practice itself. Given the fundamentally fantastic nature of these handbooks (particularly cookbooks, but perhaps this applies more generally), it is hardly surprising that these texts express anxieties about (or just play with notions of) authenticity, with a current spate of books about 'real food' or telling us 'how to eat'.

Another route for a poetics of leisure is to look for the same characteristic kinds of contradiction that we see for example in Romantic and Modernist literature. Some leisure activities seek out liminal zones. Within a few decades of 'Dover Beach', going to the seaside and while on the beach being an individual surrounded by a mass of people would become a popular mass leisure activity. The first August Bank Holiday was in 1871, four years after the publication of 'Dover Beach'. Soon there would be a mass one-day migration to the string of seaside resorts on the south coast from Margate to Torquay, with Dover itself a major town and a resort. The liminality of the beach is always a possibility; does 'going to the seaside' exploit or ignore this liminality? We would need specific studies to establish this, to find out whether something special happens in the area between land and sea, which allows the development of rewarding cognitive contradictions to make going to the seaside a practice which is 'good to think'. Here, for example, is evidence that a trip to the seaside could be an intense and profound experience, from a letter written by Anna Seward in 1793:

> ... resolved to taste, amidst the incumbent gloom of a very lowering night, a scene congenial to my taste for the terrible graces.... As I passed along the sands, the tide twice left its white surf upon my feet; and the vast curve of those fierce waves, that burst down with deafening roar, scarce three yards from me, sufficiently gratified my rage for the terrific.
> (Letters Written between the Years 1784-1807 Edinburgh 1811 III 290. July 29, 1793 (quoted Monk 1960; 214))

Also around the publication date of 'Dover Beach', organized sports were making it increasingly possible to be an individual in a crowd as specifically part of a leisure activity: the Football Association was founded 1863 with the first FA Cup in 1871, the first county cricket championship was in 1873, and the English Rugby football union was founded in 1871. Here is Walter Benjamin (1983: 61) on crowds and the experience of profound insight:

> Hugo, on the other hand, writes, 'The depths are crowds' ('Les profondeurs sont des multitudes'), and thereby gives an enormous scope to his thinking. The natural-supernatural which affected Hugo in the form of the crowd presents itself in the forest, in the animal kingdom, and by the surging sea; in any of those places the physiognomy of the big city can flash for a few moments.

Various kinds of characteristic complexity are immanent in many kinds of leisure activity. Activities which involve being alone in the countryside – hillwalking, birdwatching, fishing – all recall Romantic modes of the sublime. Activities which involve mimicry such as model-building have the potential for contradictions in scale which parallel in inverted forms the contradictions between the individual and the giant object (Saint Peter's, the Alps, the ocean) celebrated by collectors of sublime experiences. Whether these kinds of complexity are realized and experienced is a matter for empirical study.

Thus leisure activities are composed in part from the characteristically complex kinds of content which are 'good to think'. In the first part of this paper I suggested that form can also be complex, and that complex form is also 'good to think'. An appropriate question therefore is whether leisure pursuits have or are capable of having complex form. The three kinds of form I identified in verse are pattern (fitting a template), division into parts, and genre. All three are capable of being implied (though some aspects of pattern are constitutive in metrical verse). Do these kinds of form hold of leisure pursuits? As an example, consider birdwatching, a popular leisure activity in the United Kingdom. Pattern and fit to a template is involved in the identification of a bird (by matching specific parts of a bird to specific parts of a description or picture). Division into parts is also partly realized by the division of the bird into identification parts, but it is also a matter of identifying the bird as a specific kind of bird. Finally, genre might involve the self-identification of the birdwatcher as for example 'birder' (interested in looking at any bird) or 'twitcher' (interested specifically in rarities). And generic issues also arise in distinguishing birds which one watches from those which one does not; for a birdwatcher certain birds basically do not count as birds – dead birds, birds in a zoo, domestic birds (no bird guide includes the domestic hen), and exotic birds which have escaped or been released from a special collection. In all cases we are talking about form. In some cases the form holds of the birds themselves, and while this form relates to constitutive form (the bird has wings, different parts of the wing are anatomically distinct), form as it enters into birdwatching is not obviously the constitutive anatomical form of the bird. Birdwatching is not ornithology. Instead birdwatching exploits a conventionalized kind of form. The birdwatching notion of 'jizz' (general impression of shape and size) exemplifies this quite well; a skilled birdwatcher will be able to tell quickly what bird he or she is looking at by matching various aspects of the bird to a set of known categories, coresponding somehow to the perceptual 'feel' of the bird. Identification by jizz is an inferential procedure. The relevant question for our purposes is whether these kinds of 'birdwatching form', given their generally implied rather than constitutive nature, can thereby be complex in the ways characteristic of implied form in verse: vague or indeterminate, ambiguous or contradictory. If so, we might ask whether these kinds of complexity can be part of the experience of birdwatching, thus giving us one reason to say that birdwatching has an aesthetic and that we could construct a poetics for it.

It is clear that complexity is immanent in birdwatching. Foucault shows us this with his example from Borges of the classification of animals (Foucault 1970; xv): any classificatory system contains the seeds of its own destruction, particularly when that classification is built from implied rather than constitutive form. Birdwatchers arguably seek to exclude complexity by making specific identifications, but to focus too strongly on this would be to see birdwatching as a goal-driven activity rather than as a process. Equally we might understand birdwatchers as seeking out complexity in order to control and reduce it, but at the same time always looking out for new kinds of complexity; the pattern is analogous to claims made by gestaltist aestheticians that for example the metrical line works by building up and then resolving formal complexities (Bever 1986). If we take a process-oriented view of this, then there is a contradiction between complexity and simplicity, between not-knowing and knowing, which is constantly renewed. Another complexity comes from the question of whether or not one has 'spotted' a bird: there are gaps between seeing or hearing a bird and recognizing what it is, and classification is not terminal, in the sense that after the initial identification one might further identify gender or age or subspecies. One of the interesting questions about poetic form is whether there is a finite inventory of kinds of poetic form; if form is implied, the answer is that poetic form is probably infinitely variable. The same applies to classificatory form for birds, and we should acknowledge the possibility that these kinds of classificatory openness are part of the pleasure and rewards of birdwatching.

This brings us back to the issue of emergent form. If form is implied then it can be emergent. To a certain extent leisure pursuits appear to be conservative with regard to form, and one of the many functions of the handbooks and guides which accompany leisure pursuits is to provide a stock of ready-made forms. But again there is an empirical issue here; my suspicion is that for an individual who pursues a hobby or leisure activity, they have their own modes of operation which can be understood as their own emergent kinds of form. Birdwatching guides suggest certain ways of watching birds, the steps which should be followed, how to write down what you have seen, and how to take photographs. But it is possible that these rules of operation are re-imagined by actual users, for whom the rules of their own activity are emergent, changing and complex, aware of the externally prescribed rules but also working away from them. There is an analogy here with handbooks of poetic form: it is possible to look up the rules for a sonnet, and most poets who write sonnets know these rules. But the implied forms which hold of a sonnet – its genre itself, its formal organization – will often be emergent for the text, not quite fitting the rule book.

I have suggested that leisure pursuits have immanent complexity. This complexity involves how the leisure pursuits are thought, what inferences take place, and how those inferences compete with one another. Complexity in both form and content are alike: both arise as part of the pragmatic process. As a final piece of evidence for these immanent complexities, and as another route for the examination of the poetics of leisure, we might consider the high-art adaptations and versions of leisure activities. Particularly in the more recent modes of environmental art and installation art, many leisure activities are transformed into clearly aesthetic practices, offered explicitly to an audience by an artist. These aesthetic practices exploit the immanent complexities of the leisure activities themselves and can be seen as explorations of the poetics of leisure. Thus for example we might consider Hans Waanders's work on kingfishers (Danish 'Isfugl') and more generally the Alcedinidae bird family. Waanders takes the practices of birdwatchers and alters them. Thus for example 'Perches' is a collection of photographs of streams over which twigs and other perches protrude, places where kingfishers might sit. There are no actual kingfishers in the pictures, and the perches have been inserted into the bank by the photographer. We might take this as a comment on two aspects of birdwatching: its scopophilic aspects (particularly the desire to see the kingfisher, one of the most beautiful birds in Europe), and the fact of absence. For birdwathers, most of the time, the bird is absent; the play of absence and presence is part of the pleasure of the pursuit (which is why birdwatchers do not go to the zoo).

Many artists work with the notion of collecting and organizing – fundamental to many leisure pursuits; these include Peter Greenaway, Annette Messager, Andy Warhol, and so on. Here the Foucaultian possibilities, the complexities which come when we try to order things, are brought fully into the open. Other leisure pursuits have their own artists. Thus gardening is fully aestheticized by Iain Hamilton Finlay (Abrioux 1982); hillwalking and hiking are fully aestheticized by Richard Long (Long 2000). I suggest that in all cases the artists seize upon complexities – in form and content – which are immanent in the leisure pursuits, and work them through systematically for an audience.

We know that leisure pursuits are rewarding, but the question is whether they are cognitively rewarding because of their complexities in content and in form. Cultural stereotypes of more or less any leisure activity represent them as limiting and narrow, and more generally from the outside many leisure activities seem closed, finite, seeking simplicity rather than complexity, ways of escaping rather than productive pursuits. In this section I have suggested that this may be the wrong way to think about the rewards of leisure, and that leisure pursuits can have a kind of complexity analogous to that found in high art; thus we can have a poetics of leisure.

Conclusion
This paper was part of a conference on the future of Modern Language Studies, and in particular related to the question of whether cultural studies can help renew Modern Language Studies, and its subdisciplines. I have suggested that linguistics (specifically linguistic pragmatics) offers us a unified way of understanding form and content, and a way of understanding how form and content can be experienced as complex. I suggested that literary texts, a traditional subject of analysis in Modern Language Studies exemplify these kinds of complexity. I then suggested that other cultural activities also exemplify the same kinds of complexity, and cited leisure pursuits as an example. This means that it should be possible to have a poetics of leisure, informed by linguistic pragmatics. Leisure pursuits are part of what a culture is, and are also often specific to particular cultures. I have suggested that they are also a legitimate focus of academic study, and that they offer us the possibility of productive and interesting study with potentially diverse and rich outcomes.

References
Abrioux, Yves: 1992. *Ian Hamilton Finlay. A visual primer by Yves Abrioux.* Second edition. London, Reaktion Books.

Bauman, R., & Briggs, C. L. : 1990. "Poetics and performance as critical perspectives on language and social life". *Annual Review of Anthropology,* 19, pp. 59-88.

Bauman, Richard : 1975. "Verbal art as performance". *American Anthropologist,* 77, pp. 290-311.

Benjamin, Walter: 1983. *Charles Baudelaire. A Lyric Poet in the Era of High Capitalism.* London, Verso.

Bever, T. G.: 1986. "The aesthetic basis for cognitive structures". In: M. Brand & R. Harnish (Eds.), *The representation of knowledge and belief* (pp. 314-356). Tucson, University of Arizona Press.

Dorsch, T. S.: 1965. *Aristotle, Horace, Longinus. Classical Literary Criticism.* Translated by T.S. Dorsch. London, Penguin.

Fabb, Nigel: 2002a. "The metres of 'Dover Beach'". *Language and Literature,* 11, 2, pp. 111-129.

Fabb, Nigel: 2002b. *Language and Literary Structure: The linguistic analysis of form in verse and narrative.* Cambridge, Cambridge University Press.

Foucault, Michel: 1974. *The Order of Things. An Archaeology of the Human Sciences.* London, Tavistock.

Huizinga, Johan: 1938. *Homo Ludens.* Haarlem. (trans. 1949 *Homo Ludens : a study of the play-element in culture.* London, Routledge & Kegan Paul).

Jakobson, Roman: 1960. "Closing statement: Linguistics and poetics". In: Sebeok, T. (ed.) *Style in Language*, pp. 350-377. Cambridge MA, MIT Press.

Jameson, Fredric: 1981. *The Political Unconscious. Narrative as a Socially Symbolic Act*. London, Methuen.

Kant, Immanuel: 1952 [1790]. *Critique of Aesthetic Judgement*. Oxford, Oxford University Press.

Long, Richard: 2000. www.richardlong.org

Monk, S. H.: 1960. *The sublime : a study of critical theories in eighteenth century England*. University of Michigan Press.

Sperber, Dan and Wilson, Deirdre: 1995. *Relevance: Communication and Cognition*. 2nd edition. Oxford, Blackwell.

Sperber, Dan: 1975. *Rethinking Symbolism*. Cambridge, Cambridge University Press.

Venturi, Robert: 1977. *Complexity and contradiction in architecture*. London, Architectural Press.

Thanks to Hans Lauge Hansen, Janet Fabb, Elspeth Findlay, Murray Pittock, and participants at the conference.

Translation Studies:
From Linguistics and Beyond and Back Again[1]

by
Hanne Jansen
University of Copenhagen

As the title of this section indicates, we understand translation – both translational practice and the study of this practice – as a privileged interface between linguistics, literary studies and cultural studies. In view of the many and very different approaches to translation practised by scholars today, it is clear that translation as a field of research is positioned between various disciplines. In the following, I will present a survey on some of the most important trends in Translation Studies which have emerged within the last 50 years, concluding with a brief account of my own mainly linguistically based work. Making such a survey is however by no means an easy matter. The study of translation practice and the theoretical reflections on the nature of translation is no longer seen as an ancillary or subordinate activity within linguistics or literary studies. Yet the various approaches to Translation Studies are sometimes so different, their points of departure so far from each other, and their conclusions and ways of implementing their reflections so contrasting, that it is difficult to glimpse any unifying elements. In fact, even when speaking as an advocate of ranking Translation Studies as an autonomous discipline, Susan Bassnett draws attention to its underlying interdisciplinary nature by pointing out the very complexity and ramification of the field (cf. Susan Bassnett 1991; 1).

The field of Translation Studies is thus on the one hand a discipline in its own right, that is, a research area with a well-defined and distinct subject matter (translation as process and as product), and a series of concepts,

---

[1] The first part of the following contribution is to some extent a reproposing of some reflections presented in a paper at the VI Congresso degli Italianisti Scandinavi, Lund, 16-18 August 2001. This paper, entitled "Traduzione e traduttologia: campo di ricerca e disciplina didattica", is due to be published later in 2002.

problems and perspectives which have to be taken into account and to be reflected upon (the notion of equivalence, the role of the translator, the status of the original text, the translation norms, the process of translation etc.). On the other hand, it is an object of study where different disciplines (linguistics, psychology, literary criticism, anthropology, cultural studies etc.) can legitimately meet (that is, without "converting" to Translation Studies) in profitable discussion, each applying its specific specialised knowledge to the further understanding of what goes on in translating and translations and how these interact with literature and society in general.

I will begin my survey in the 1950s. For at least two thousands years, writers, philosophers and scholars have discussed what translation is all about and how good translations should be produced, thereby formulating many of the central queries and issues within modern Translation Studies. Nevertheless it is only from about the middle of the last century that scholars began to assemble these very relevant and very perspicacious, but until then rather sporadic reflections, and subject them to a more theoretically grounded and terminologically consistent analysis: in other words, to treat them as science. To start with, the theoretical basis was clearly linguistic: attention was primarily directed towards the language system, especially the typological and structural differences between languages, with the focus on rather small and bounded linguistic units. At the risk of seeming banal, it is worth mentioning that in the 1950s and the 1960s Translation Studies were very often linked to attempts to operationalise computerised or automatic translation, and thereby to formulate machine-readable rules of transposition from one language into another.[2]

Two important works from this first linguistic phase of Translation Studies which both have a prevailing interest for comparing the formal structures of source language (SL) and target language (TL), are Vinay & Darbelnet's *Stylistique comparé du français et de l'anglais* from 1958, and Catford's *A Linguistic Theory of Translation* from 1965. Vinay & Darbelnet proposed seven translation strategies, relating respectively to direct or literal translation and to oblique translation, for example "transposition, which involves replacing one word class with another without changing the meaning of the message" (Vinay & Darbelnet 1958/2000; 8); although from both a lexical and a structural point of view they all operate on single words or expressions which are very delimited, and do not extend beyond the boundaries of the sentence. Catford, too, distinguishes between literal, or "bounded" and free, or "unbounded" translation. His aim is to establish a "taxonomy" of translation equivalences, by setting up different kinds of "shifts", seen as "departures from formal correspondence in the process of

---

[2] The research on machine translation is still a very important area, but does not at present relate to the general field of Translation Studies.

going from the SL to the TL" (Catford 1965/2000; 141).[3] The translation equivalence may involve level-shifts (from grammar to lexis, or vice versa), rank-shifts (from sentence to clause, or group, or word, or even morpheme), structure-shifts (that is, re-ordering within the syntactic construction), class-shifts, and other kind of shifts. The translation unit involved in these shifts, however, falls entirely within the scope of the sentence – a fact revealed in an almost surprised footnote noticing that in translation from German into English equivalence may frequently be established between a single sentence and a unit greater than the sentence, i.e. the paragraph (Catford 1965/2000; 147).

In the course of the 1970s, with the rise of sociolinguistics, pragmatics, textlinguistics, etc., the focus changed from language system to language usage, from abstract sentences to concrete utterances or speech acts, from the ideal language-user to the specific relationship between sender and addressee. The general transition in linguistics from a formalist to a functionalist paradigm is paralleled by the expansion of the translation unit, the scope shifting from the sentence to the text: the text seen as an organised structure governed by such factors as cohesion, coherence and other linguistic phenomena which link the smaller units to their immediate cotext and to the text as a whole; and the text seen as language put to use in a specific context, that is, a specific communicative situation, with all the pragmatic, sociological and, last but not least, text-typological implications this situation entails. An important contribution is Katharina Reiss' *Texttyp und Übersetzungsmethode* from 1976, that places the search for translation strategies and translation equivalence at the level of texts and text types.

Although some of the earliest attempts to set up text typologies tend to be rather structuralist and formalist in their approach (cf. Egon Werlich and his *Typologie der Texte* from 1975), it is difficult to avoid reflections on the function of the text, whether the focus is on the cognitive mode, the institutional role, the membership in a literary genre, or other parameters. Within the framework of translation, comparability and equivalence of different text types across the linguistic borders became a question of crucial importance.

The question of equivalence becomes even more crucial as during the 1980s the translation unit underwent a further expansion from the text and its immediate context to the general context, i.e. to its cultural and historical setting. This transition within Translation Studies is often men-

---

[3] When Crisafulli (1993; 195) sets out to "determine the validity of this theory [Catford's linguistic theory of translation] in terms of its explanatory power and to consider whether other considerations than Catford's are necessary to a satisfactory theory of translation", it may be added that Catford's theory is meant to provide an account of "how" rather than an explanation of "why".

tioned as "the Cultural Turn" and is by many scholars viewed as far more decisive than the above-mentioned expansion of the translation unit from word or sentence to text (cf. Lefevere & Bassnett 1990; 4).

In this view translation is seen as a meeting, a confrontation, a transposition, no longer between two languages or between two texts, but between two cultures: Translation is an act of intercultural communication or mediation. As Edoardo Crisafulli says (1993: 204-205):

> The contribution of the cultural approach to a comprehensive theory of translation is that, at least as far as literary translations are concerned, translation does not take place in a vacuum.

Both source text and target text are situated in a specific cultural setting, and as such are historically, socially and ideologically determined. A text is a historical testimony, an expression of a specific culture, a specific *Weltanschauung*. What is emphasised by the Cultural Turn is the cultural setting of the target text, and especially the function of the translated text in this new setting. This is the central question put forward by the Skopos Theory (introduced by Reiss & Vermeer 1984), and it entails serious implications for the seemingly inevitable, but at the same time highly problematic, notion of equivalence. As seen in the previous paragraph, the notion of equivalence presupposes an ideal, or at least a desirable, relationship of similarity, symmetry, parity, sameness between the source text and the target text. But similarity or symmetry with regard to what? What is going to be held constant or similar in the process of translation? The form, the content, a specific linguistic level or a specific level of meaning (the referential, the expressive, the cognitive, the phatic, etc.)? As pointed out by Ingemai Larsen in her contribution "Translation and Cultural History", equivalence may be defined as making available for the target group "the same message and the same experience" as was available for the addressee of the original text - a definition which, however, remains open to many interpretations. The Skopos Theory somewhat mercilessly raises doubts about the notion of equivalence itself, about the legitimacy and the appropriateness of this notion in discussing translation quality. Equivalence is dethroned from its traditional position, and subordinated instead to the notion of adequacy, cf. Gutt (1991; 16):

> One of the most developed and explicit attempts to set up an evaluative framework for translation that goes beyond statements about equivalence is the action-theoretic approach developed by Reiss and Vermeer (1984) (...) they suggest that equivalence is, in fact, only a special case of a more general notion: that of adequacy. Adequacy in turn is always linked to the notion of purpose ('skopos') - and it is this notion that dominates translation.

This new parameter in the discussion of translation processes and translation quality depends almost entirely on the function that the target text is intended to perform in its new historical and cultural context. The notion of adequacy thus detaches the translation much more from the original text and the original author than the notion of equivalence, which – whatever the size of the translation unit – is always based on some kind of comparison (structural, semantic, communicative) between two languages or two texts .

A further step into the cultural domain, parting translation from the notion of equivalence and the original text, is taken by the so-called Manipulation School (which has as a kind of "manifesto" the anthology *The Manipulation of Literature* edited by Theo Hermanns in 1985), seeing - cf. Bassnett (1991; xvii):

> (...) translation as one of the processes of literary manipulation, whereby texts are rewritten across linguistic boundaries and that rewriting takes place in a very clearly inscribed cultural and historical context.

Translation, in this view, is literary manipulation - like literary criticism, text editing, etc. – in which the original is rewritten and recontextualised. The focus is placed on the translator as "text operator": s/he is a member of the target culture, sharing the systems of values, beliefs and knowledge of that culture at that specific historical moment, including literary norms and other rules and standards regarding text production.

The act of translating is described with new metaphors, substituting for example the traditional image of translation as a "reflection" of the source text, with the less innocent, but far more realistic metaphor of "refraction", cf. Bassnett (1991; xvii):

> A reflection involves a mirroring, a copy of an original; a refraction involves changes of perception, and this is an image that is useful to describe what happens when a text crosses from one culture to another. Moreover, refraction theory necessarily involves a consideration of literary evolution and thus places translation in a time continuum...[4]

Another even more subversive metaphor for the translator as text operator is that of the "cannibal", cf. Bassnett (1991; xv):

> Brazilian translators have introduced a new metaphor (...) the image of the translator as cannibal, devouring the source text in a ritual that results in the creation of something completely new (...) The cannibalistic notion of translation involves a changed idea of the value of the original text in relation to its reception in the target culture (...) linked to the view of translation propounded by Jacques Derrida, when he argues that the translation process creates an 'original' text, the opposite of the traditional position whereby the 'original' is the starting point.

---

[4] The same or at least a similar metaphor is found in the title of a recent (1999) Danish anthology on literary translation, *Glas kaster skygge* (Glass throws a shadow).

The cannibalistic image fits in fact very well with the deconstructivist or post-structuralist view of literature, where intertextuality is seen as a fundamental factor in all acts of producing and decoding texts: no text is completely new, in that every single text is influenced by and produced in the light of other texts; but at the same time all texts are in a sense equally new, translations as well as other texts, and thus the traditional hierarchy of original-translation as original-copy falls apart, cf. the quotation of Octavio Paz in Bassnett (1991; 38):

> All texts, he [Octavio Paz] claims, are 'translations of translations of translations': Every text is unique and, at the same time, it is the translation of another text. No text is entirely original (...) However, this argument can be turned around without losing any of its validity: all texts are original because every translation is distinctive. Every translation, up to a certain point, is an invention and as such it constitutes a unique text.

Following the notion of "dialogism" proposed by Bakhtin, translations can be seen as a dialogue with the original text, just as the original can be seen as a dialogue with an infinite number of preceding texts. And the parallel does not stop here: the original text is not just a response to other texts, but a response to "being" itself: every text is an attempt to translate the non-verbal into language (cf. a survey of Octavio Paz', Derrida's and Backtin's reflections on translation in Lindegaard 1997).

In comparison with the far more practical knowledge aimed at in the linguistically based studies mentioned above, the view of translation propagated by these literary scholars has taken quite a metaphysical turn. Carried to its extreme, this view generates a new principle of untranslatability. The "traditional" Sapir-Whorff Hypothesis of untranslatability is based on linguistic relativism, that is - cf. Malmkjær (1991; 306-308):

> (...) a person's native language sets up a series of categories which act as a pair of grid spectacles through which s/he views the world; it categorizes experience for the speakers of the language (...) Sapir omits the possibility of translation altogether in statements like the following: 'No two languages are ever sufficiently similar to be considered as representing the same social reality. The worlds in which different societies live are distinct worlds, not merely the same world with different labels attached'.

The deconstructivist, or postmodern principle of untranslatability is based instead on what we could call interpretative or hermeneutic relativism: as quoted above, all texts are equally original and autonomous, or equally "recycled" and dependent on other texts. Without some kind of *tertium comparationis* to be found outside the text itself, without some criteria for establishing equivalence, the original text and the translated text become incommensurable, cf. Pedersen (1997; 66):

> With the postmodernist approach (...) we have returned to the doctrine of untranslatability. To the postmodernist, everything is text - they are not

interested in the reference of texts to the extralinguistic world, because they do not believe that we can understand or perceive that world except through language - and to them all text is literature or metaphor.

The emphasis that modern literary studies, and not merely the deconstructivists, put on the role of the reader not only as a decoder of the meaning of the text, but also as an active collaborator in establishing and creating this very meaning, has implications for the role of the translator as well, as the following passage underlines, cf. Bassnett (1991; 79):

> (...) Julia Kristeva sees the reader as realizing the expansion of the work's process of semiosis. The reader, then, *translates* or *decodes* the text according to a different set of systems and the idea of the one 'correct' reading is dissolved (...) Quite clearly, the idea of the reader as translator and the enormous freedom this vision bestows must be handled responsibly.

The idea of one 'correct' reading disintegrates, and so, consequently, does the idea of one 'correct' translation. The translator is no longer an invisible presence, but inevitably leaves his or her mark on the text, manipulates it, even distorts it; what is more important, s/he is not simply bound, but also entitled, to do so.

The freedom and, as the quotation says, the responsibility that is bestowed on the translator can seem quite frightening, both to the translator him/herself, and to the readers for whom the translation is intended. It is therefore reassuring that it is pointed out that: "The translator's freedom is limited" (Jakobsen 1993; 163). In fact, translations, like all other texts, have intertextual relationships with other texts, but – cf. Jakobsen (ibid):

> (...) unlike nearly all other types of text, however, a translation always has a unique intertextual relationship with another text, viz. the source language text of which it is the target language version. It is this unique or privileged intertextual relationship which most obviously defines the possibilities and the limits of the translator's work and makes translation a special kind of text production method.

This might seem a banal truth, but evidently is not so, seeing the need to make a point of it. In a similar way Crisafulli, a translation theoretician who has worked within the framework of the Manipulation School, brings the focus back to the original text, cf. Crisafulli (2001; 1):

> Translation is not only (or simply) a form of 'manipulation' (Bassnett-Lefevere 1990: vii), or 'ethnocentric assimilation' (Venuti 1996: 93); it is, first and foremost, interpretation."

The very notion of manipulation presupposes that the source text has, in some way, an "essential", "true", "correct" meaning that may, but not necessarily, be manipulated by the reader or translator; this view, in turn, clashes with the post-structuralist perspective that posits a text's meaning as more or less arbitrarily constructed by the interpreter. But as Umberto

Eco says, there are limits to interpretation, and Crisafulli, who leans on Eco's hermeneutic theory, seeks criteria that make it possible "to distinguish between legitimate interpretations, which bring out the meaning potential in the source text, and instances of over-interpretation" (Crisafulli 2001; 7).

An even more categorical refusal of the above-mentioned views - especially when emphasis is put on the target culture, the purpose of the translation, the intercultural mediation - is presented by the adherents of more traditional hermeneutic approaches, anchored in the reflections of Schleiermacher, Heidegger and Gadamer – cf. Stolze (2001; 3):

> There is no such thing as a "transfer", but the cognitive representation of the message links the translation to the original (...) there is no bargaining about a translation's "skopos", since it is not the target culture that determines the perception of the original message (...) Translation is a matter of writing [so to create "presence" for the original message], not so much of intercultural comparison.

In other words, the translator does not have licence to change the text by cultural filtering or adaptation; to bring the text to the reader, that is, to "naturalise" it, is to violate the sanctity of the original. Stolze, nonetheless, adds (ibid.) that this "creating presence" for the message "will of course be done in an idiomatic way so that target readers may easily understand it". That it should be taken for granted that idiomaticity is a goal in translations is not however the case. In fact, in a very complex and metaphysical, if not mystical, piece of writing on translation (the introduction to the translation of Baudelaire's *Tableux Parisiens*, 1923), Walter Benjamin sees the act of translation as an important expression of the striving towards a pure language[5], and advocates strongly for literal or overt translation, cf. Benjamin (1923/2000; 21):

> Therefore it is not the highest praise of a translation, particularly in the age of its origin, to say that it reads as if it had originally been written in that language. Rather, the significance of fidelity as ensured by literalness is that the work reflects the great longing for linguistic complementation. A real translation is transparent; it does not cover the original, does not black its light, but allows the pure language, as though reinforced by its own medium to shine upon the original all the more fully.

The next contribution by Lene Waage Petersen on "Literary Translations between Philology and Aesthetics" will comment further on the translator as reader and interpreter, on different kinds of reading and interpretation, and on balance between freedom and fidelity *vis-à-vis* the original text

---

[5] Cf. Benjamin (1923/2000; 22): "In this pure language - which no longer means or expresses anything but is, as expressionless and creative Word, that which is meant in all languages - all information, all sense, and all intention - finally encounter a stratum in which it is destined to be extinguished."

which is involved in all translating, and especially when working with literary texts.

Although it is possible to present objections to some of the more radical positions and implications of the Manipulation School, and this has certainly been done, this approach has in my opinion a very important point in seeing both the making of literature and the translation of literature as a "political factor", something determined by relations of power, both cultural, social and ideological, but at the same time determining the very same relations: to work with literary texts, whether as writer, scholar, critic or translator, is by no means an innocent activity, cf. Lefevere & Bassnett (1990; 12):

> They [the constraints in the process of the writing and rewriting of texts] ultimately have to do with power and manipulation, two issues potentially of enormous interest not only to those engaged in literary studies, but also to all their victims outside.

The political and ethical facets of translation are all the more evident when the translating takes place in a post-colonial context, when the translator is working on or within a minority language – as Ingemai Larsen will show us below – or when the object of study is the relationship between gender, language and translation.

Though the theories that have dominated Translation Studies in the past decades have emphasised, on the one hand, culture, context and communication[6], and, on the other, deconstruction, dialogism and intertextuality, this does not mean that linguistics as a discipline has taken no interest in translation. On the contrary, almost all the most important trends within modern linguistics have been exploited in translation practice and theory, cf. *Cognitive linguistics and poetics of translation* (1993) by Elisabeth Tabakowska, *Translation and Relevance* (1991) by Ernst-August Gutt, or *Cross-cultural Pragmatics and Translation* (2002) by Juliane House, just to mention a few.

It would furthermore seem that Translation Studies are, at least to some extent, turning the focus "back" to the linguistic dimension, without, however, putting aside the insights gained by the studies of the broader pragmatic, hermeneutic and cultural context of text and translation. As Crisafulli puts it (Crisafulli 1993; 205-206):

> Although I advocate the validity of such a perspective [the cultural approach], I also wish to stress that the linguistic dimension of enquiry is fundamental

---

[6] Cf. what might be said to be the ultimate expansion of the scope of translation, "The Translation Turn in Cultural Studies", as is stated in the title of one of Susan Bassnett's latest contributions (Bassnett 2000).

> (...) such an analysis [a linguistic one] takes the data as its starting point, and the primary data in translations are linguistic.

A recent and very productive trend within Translation Studies is the corpus-based translation studies introduced in the 1990s by Mona Baker, a trend which is in fact more linguistically and empirically founded; cf. the following quotation from a newsletter distributed by the European Society for Translation Studies (EST) summing up the major issues presented at a conference on translation research in Copenhagen, August 2001:

> The rapidly growing popularity of corpora studies is striking in a field largely dominated by theory in the literary and cultural tradition so far (...) Not so long ago, criticism was aimed at those who called for more empirical research for allegedly disregarding theory. The pendulum swings.[7]

Corpus-based studies, using large electronic corpora consisting of translated texts and original texts, aim for example at testing hypotheses on translation universals; that is - cf. Mauranen (2000; 120):

> (...) 'translation universals', i.e. linguistic properties which characterize translations independently of the particular language pair involved or particular circumstances of the translation processes (...) translation universals, such as explicitation, simplification, levelling-out and conventionalization. (see e.g. Baker 1996)

The corpora can be used to detect characteristic features of translated language within specific genres, as well as the occurrence of distinctive lexical or syntactic choices, phenomena of repetition etc., or to describe the language of individual literary translators, comparing for example the degree of his/hers creativity within the target language to that of not-translated literary texts - cf. Mona Baker (2000): *Towards a Methodology for Investigating the Style of a Literary Translator*.

Finally, the very eliciting of corpora based on translations can be regarded as a revaluation and rehabilitation of translated language. In the huge text corpora which are being collected in many countries at present, translated texts are very seldom included, on the grounds that, cf. Mauranen (2000; 139) "they do not reflect 'the language' correctly (whatever that

---

[7] George Steiner, one of the central figures within the Hermeneutic Movement, distinguishes between "four historical periods of translation theory, characterised by:
> 1. An immediate empirical focus (from Antiquity through the close of the 18th century)
> 2. A hermeneutic approach (lasting until the mid-1940s)
> 3. A more or less purely linguistic approach (until approximately the 1970s)
> 4. A reversion to hermeneutic and almost metaphysical inquiries into translation and interpretation." (cf. Lindegaaard 1997; 70)

We may now be entering a new "linguistic period".

beast might be, if it excludes major variants like translations)". A quite significant exclusion, considering that a substantial part of the linguistic input we are subject to in everyday life is, as a matter of fact, translated language.

My survey of "that vastly complex field with many far-reaching ramifications" (Bassnett 1991; 1) that constitutes Translation Studies is coming to an end. One of the most evident changes within this field of research in the last five decades has been its moving from a strictly linguistic perspective to reflections which reached far beyond the language dimension, as the contributions of Lene Waage Petersen and Ingemai Larsen will demonstrate in more detail. As said above, however, it seems that lately a renewed interest has been taken in the linguistic material itself and in more specifically linguistic analysis.[8] In this spirit, and as a conclusion, I will turn briefly to my own work, which is in fact based on a linguistic approach, adding incidentally that I actually entered the field of linguistics through work with literary translation (translation into Danish of Claudio Magris' *Danubio*[9]). The act of translating – this very close, palpable and sensous meeting with a text – is indeed an incomparable eye-opener: to the aesthetic qualities of the text (even by their very eluding any attempt of translation); to the different ways we conceptualise reality and the different values we attach to our being in it; and last but not least, to the (mysterious) ways in which language works.

Translation has thus a very central role in linguistics, a role that should, in my view, be accentuated much more in the teaching of this discipline, putting the emphasis on the cognitive and communicative (and, cf. the next contribution, aesthetic) functions that language performs in real texts, and departing definitely from the construed, context-free sentences which have so often constituted the traditional bridge between translation and linguistics. That linguistics, in return, has a central role in translation, goes without saying: a full grasp of the morphologic, syntactic and semantic structures of a text is a *sine qua non* if the text – especially the literary text – is to be successfully reproposed in a new language, or if the choices made in this reproposal are to be explained, and eventually evaluated.

---

[8] Cf. Herslund (1998; 7): "Many recent studies on translation put the emphasis on the pragmatic and textual factors or on the process of translation itself. Thus the actual linguistic material risks fading into the background. The project "Linguistic Translation" aims at studying and specifying the structural and typological differences (...) and in this way anchors the act of translation in the structural differences between the languages at different levels." [my translation]

[9] Claudio Magris (1986): *Danubio*. Garzanti. Translation into Danish by Hanne Jansen (1989): *Donau*. Samleren.

My work has dealt with genre conventions in Italian and Danish respectively, and is at present concerned with comparative text typology in a more broad perspective, including standards for written and oral texts which do indeed often deviate from one language to another. This involves working with the largest linguistic unit, i.e. the text as an integral whole seen in a specific communicative and cultural setting. To define, however, what is characteristic for Italian and Danish essay texts (abstract style *versus* concrete style), or what constitute distinctive features in oral and written text in the two languages, it is necessary to have a "close encounter" with the raw linguistic material, that is, the structural and functional elements found in the specific text. In this respect, my research focuses on very small linguistic units, relating as it does to the significance of word classes in text and translation. The changes in the frequency and distribution of different word classes that inevitably take place when translating, is indeed a classical theme within translation studies, cf. the strategy of transposition of Vinay & Darbelnet and the class shifts of Catford. I am, however, interested not so much in the shifts themselves but in the decisive and far-reaching implications those changes have for the text as a whole, not least when working on literary texts. This includes implications for the texture of the text: which linguistic "bricks" are used determines the distribution and grouping of the content elements in the textual sequence; it determines the informational flow and density, the rhythm, the pauses, the "intonational" patterns put into the text (whether written or oral[10]); it determines the on-going processing of the text by the reader, and thereby captures or reproposes the author's/narrator's voice[11]. It also includes implications for the images, the mental representations that the text evokes in the mind of the reader: the word classes are defined, in fact, not only, and maybe not primarily, on the basis of their syntactic properties, but on the basis of their meaning, of their signifying something; and in this area, the semantics of word classes, I believe that Cognitive Grammar provides a very useful framework.

One of the crucial claims set forward by Cognitive Grammar - here I am referring primarily to R.W. Langacker - is the intimate relationship between the categories involved in the way we perceive reality (through our senses and our body), in the way we conceptualise reality (in our minds) and in the way we express reality (with our language). Word classes (at least the most basic and recurrent ones) can thus be defined according to their prototypical use in coding distinctive features of (our perception of) a

---

[10] Cf. the next contribution of Lene Waage Petersen, that emphasizes the importance of reading aloud.

[11] Cf. Newmark (1981): "Grammatical meaning is more significant (the 'tone' or 'flavour' of the text, its primary aspect, is perhaps dictated by its syntax), less precise, more general and sometimes more elusive than lexical meaning."

typical, basic event or situation. Verbs thus prototypically code temporal relations between entities (processes), nouns code the entities participating in a relation (things), prepositions spatial relations between entities, and so forth. This prototypical use of word classes can of course be "overruled" in the specific utterance or text, that is, the "conceived situation" may be "construed" in a not prototypical way[12], whether due to the nature of the event to be depicted, to the perspective adopted towards this event, or to the pragmatic and/or cognitive mode of the text.[13] But by virtue of the word class-membership itself, even when overruled - a typical instance is verbal nouns - the prototypical use still lingers on as a core meaning of the word, having an impact on the mental image evoked by the word and consequently on the overall semantic and conceptual output of the text.

As stated above, changes in word class patterns are inevitable in translation. A translator working from Italian into Danish very often (especially within certain text types and genres, as for instance essay texts) finds him/herself compelled to render the above-mentioned verbal nouns with the corresponding non-derivative verbs. Thereby s/he does not only disturb the texture and rhythm of the text, but actually interferes with the very core of the semantic or cognitive structure of the text, evoking mental images of temporal relations rather than of entities. In a similar way, when a translator from Danish to Italian, in the re-rendering of movement processes, turns analytical verbal constructs such as verb + spatial particle (*gå ind/ ud/ op/ ned* = go in/ out/ up/ down) into synthetic verbs that express the direction of movement within the verbal root (*entrare, uscire, salire, scendere* = enter, exit, ascend, descend), this significantly changes the degree of emphasis put on the spatial dimension. This means that Vinay & Darbelnet's definition of a word class change as a "transposition, which involves replacing one word class with another without changing the meaning of the message" does not hold – the meaning does change.

---

[12] For a detailed description of the notion of "construal", that is, "the ability of speakers to construe the same basic situation in many different ways, i.e. to structure it by means of alternate images", see Langacker (1987; 116-117), and on the usefulness in Translation Studies of these notions and of others put forward by Cognitive Grammar, see Tabakowska (1993), Halverson (2001) and Jansen (1996).

[13] Cf. the notion of "grammatical metaphor" introduced by Halliday (1994; xviii): "This is how children are able to construe a grammar: because they can make a link between the categories of the grammar and the reality that is around them and inside their heads. They can see the sense that lies behind the code. Later on, they will learn the principle of "grammatical metaphor" whereby meanings may be cross-coded, phenomena represented by categories other than those evolved to represent them."

Some of these changes are due to structural or typological differences between the source language and the target language, some conform rather to general tendencies in the exploitation of the possibilities of system, and some are related to more specific differences within text typology and genre conventions. Since the latter are largely a matter of choice, and not obligatory in order to produce either a grammatical correct or an idiomatically acceptable target text, they are by far the most difficult to handle and the most open to discussion.

The relation between word classes and translation gives rise to a number of interesting questions which I will only have time to mention briefly.

Do some languages basically, that is typologically, give preference to certain word classes? - cf. the lexicalization patterns in Danish and Italian, where a general tendency in Danish calls for a more specific lexicalization of verbs as well as of spatial particles, while in Italian it is generally nouns that tend to be more specific in their signification, raising the rather suggestive hypothesis that Danish – mentally, cognitively – puts the focus on relations, and Italian on entities.[14] How can this hypothesis be applied in working with translations?

Do some genres and text types, including written *versus* oral, put more weight on some word classes than on others, cf. Italian oral texts and informal texts that make use of a larger number and greater variety of analytical verbal constructs, and thus foreground the spatial dimension to a greater extent than does written language and more formal register? How can this intra-linguistic pattern be rendered in a language and a rhetorical tradition which do not present the same variation?

And to conclude these reflections on the significance of a strict linguistic analysis with a final question, before ceding the floor to my colleagues within the literary and cultural domains: when and to what extent are word-class changes, and the interference in the semantic/cognitive core of texts implied by these changes, acceptable, even if undertaken to comply with different conventions within a particular text genre or text mode (written/oral) or register? If, as claimed here, word-class changes do indeed represent not just a structural adaptation to the target language, but also a mental and a "rhythmical" adaptation, how far can one carry this strategy of adaptation, of "naturalization", in literary translation, without jeopardising the uniqueness of the text and the "otherness" of the *Weltanschauung* which it offers its new readers?

References

Baker, Mona: 1995. "Corpora in Translation Studies: An Overview and Some Suggestions for Future Research". *Target* 7(2), pp. 223-243.

Baker, Mona: 1998. *Routledge Encyclopaedia of Translation Studies*. Routledge.

---

[14] Cf. Korzen (1998).

Baker, Mona: 2000. "Towards a Methodology for Investigating the Style of a Literary Translator". *Target* 7(2), pp. 241-266.

Bassnett, Susan: 1991 [1980]. *Translation Studies*. Revised Edition. Routledge.

Bassnett, Susan: 2000. "The Translation Turn in Cultural Studies". Chap. 8 in Bassnett & Lefevere (eds.): *Constructing Cultures. Essays on Literary Translation*. Clevedon, Multilingual Matters, pp. 123-140.

Benjamin, Walter: 1923/2000. "The task of the translator. An introduction to the translation of Baudelaire's *Tableux Parisiens*", trans. Harry Zohn, reprinted in Venuti (2000), pp. 15-25.

Catford, J.C.: 1965/2000. "Translation Shifts", Chap.12 in *A Linguistic Theory of Translation*. Reprinted in Venuti (2000), pp. 141-147.

Crisafulli, Edoardo: 1993. "Culture and text: equivalence revisited". *Perspectives: Studies in Translatology*, 1993: 2. Museum Tusculanum, pp. 194-206.

Crisafulli, Edoardo: 2001. "Umberto Eco's Hermenuetics and Translation: Between 'Manipulation' and 'Over-interpretation'". Paper from the site of the EST-conference, August 2001, at the Copenhagen Business School.

Gutt, Ernst-August: 1991. *Translation and Relevance. Cognition and Context*. Basil Blackwell.

Hallliday, M.A.K.: 1994. *An Introduction to Functional Grammar. Second Edition*. London. Edward Arnold.

Halverson, Gunver: 2001: "An outline of a cognitive theory of translation". Paper from the site of the EST-Conference, August 2001, at the Copenhagen Business School.

Hasselbach, Iben red.: (1999). *Glas kaster skygge. Om litterær oversættelse*. Gyldendal.

Herslund, Michael: 1998. "Typologi, leksikalisering og oversættelse". Herslund (red.): *Lingvistisk oversættelse*, Copenhagen Working Papers in LSP, 3-1998, pp. 7-12.

House, Juliane: 2002. "Cross-cultural pragmatics and translation". Paper given at the EU Conference *Text and Translation*, Prague, March 2002.

Jakobsen, Arnt Lykke: 1993. "Translation as textual (re)production". *Perspectives: Studies in Translatology*, 1993: 2. Museum Tusculanum, pp. 155-165.

Jansen, Hanne: 1996. "Da processo a cosa... La subordinazione vista in una prospettiva cognitiva". Lihn Jensen (ed.): *Atti del IV Congresso degli Italianisti Scandinavi, Copenhagen, 8-10 giugno 1995*. Copenhagen, Samfundslitteratur, pp. 193-212.

Jansen, Hanne: 2001. "Brøndal og Langacker. Omkring ordklassers semantik". Bache et al. (eds.): *Ny forskning i grammatik. Fællespublikation 8. Gilbjerghovedsymposiet 2000*. Odense Universitetsforlag, pp. 127-148.

Jansen, Hanne: 2002. "Spatial particles: A joint class? Reflections on the use of prepositions and locative adverbs in Danish and Italian." Paper presented at the Congress on *Adpositions of Movement*, Leuven, 14-16 January 2002.

Korzen, Iørn: 1998. "Leksikaliseringsmønstre i italiensk og dansk". Herslund (red.): *Lingvistisk oversættelse*, Copenhagen Working Papers in LSP, 3-1998, pp. 13-42.

Korzen, Iørn & Carla Marello: 2000. *Argomenti per una linguistica della traduzione / Notes pour une linguistique de la traduction / On Linguistic Aspects of Translation*. Edizioni dell'Orso.

Langacker, Ronald W.: 1987/1991. *Foundations of Cognitive Grammar. Vol.I+II*. Stanford University Press.

Lefevere, André & Susan Bassnett: 1990. "Proust's Grandmother and the Thousand and One Nights: The 'Cultural Turn' in Translation Studies". Bassnett & Lefevere (eds.): *Translation, History and Culture*. London/New York, Pinter Publishers, pp. 1-13.

Lindegaard, Annette: 1997. "Translation, Deconstruction and Dialogism". Dollerup et al. (red.): *An Introduction to Translation Studies*. København, Center for Oversættelsesvidenskab, pp. 69-82.

Malmkjær, Kirsten (ed): 1991. *The Linguistics Encyclopedia*. London/NewYork, Routledge.

Newmark, Peter: 1981. *Approaches to Translation*.

Mauranen, Anna: 2000. "Strange Strings in Translated Language. A Study on Corpora". Maeve Olohan (ed.): *Intercultural Faultlines. Research Models in Translations Studies I. Textual and Cognitive Aspects*. Manchester, St. Jerome, pp. 119-141.

Pedersen, Viggo Hjørnager: 1997. "Translation studies past and present". Dollerup et al. (red): *An Introduction to Translation Studies*. København, pp. 47-68.

Reiss, Katharina: 1976. *Texttyp und Übersetzungsmehode*. Kronberg, Scriptor.

Skytte, Gunver & Iørn Korzen: 2000. *Italiensk-dansk sprogbrug i komparativt perspektiv*. Samfundslitteratur.

Snell-Hornby, Mary: 1988. *Translation Studies. An Integrated Approach*. Amsterdam, Benjamins.

Stolze, Radegundis: 2001. "Creating 'presence' in translation". Paper from the site of the EST-conference, August 2001, at the Copenhagen Business School.

Tabakowska, Elisabeth: 1993. *Cognitive Linguistics and Poetics of Translation*. Tübingen, Gunter Narr.

Venuti, Laurence : 2000. *The Translation Studies Reader*. London/New York, Routledge.

Vinay, Jean-Paul & Jean Darbelnet: 1958/2000. "A methodology for translation" from *Stylistique comparé du francais et de l'anglais*, trans. Sager & Hamel, reprinted in Venuti (2000), pp. 84-93.

Werlich, Egon: 1975. *Typologie der Texte*. Heidelberg, Quelle & Meyer.

Literary Translations between Philology and Aesthetics

by

Lene Waage Petersen

University of Copenhagen

In the present context my contribution forms part of a triptychon consisting of literary, linguistic and cultural translation – I shall leave out of account the specific linguistic field that sees translation as a general and fundamental strategy in language acquisition. The insights that linguistically oriented work on translation is able to convey about structural, syntactic, cognitive and semantic differences are fundamental for the expansion of our linguistic consciousness and our linguistic competences. And naturally a great part of literary translation depends on linguistic competences in a wide sense.

I shall also ignore the specific cultural competences one could describe as philological, that is the comprehension of the foreign word in a broad historical and cultural context – one could (with Bakhtin) define it as a dialogue with the existing meanings and voices outside the text – a dialogue which is absolutely necessary and which constitutes a fully integrated part of the literary translation.

These are general and fundamental issues, also seen in relation to other types and genres of texts than the purely literary. Evidently literary translation (and working with literature in general) cannot take place in a void. The historical positions of the text and of the interpreter have been an integrated part of the hermeneutic approach to the understanding and translation of texts for a long time.

In this specific context I have chosen to focus on the specifically literary issues concerning translation. Naturally that requires a definition of the "specifically literary". Depending on your point of view that is either a very big question or a very simple problem. One could say that the literary consists in whatever a given period chooses to define as belonging to the field of literature. That is, a concept of literature is historically conditioned in its inclusion or exclusion of various genres of text.

One could also claim that the literary fundamentally includes texts with an aesthetic component, that is, texts in which the sensuous aspects of language are developed on the level of form and expression. In that way language becomes the object of an aesthetic adaptation and at the same time a place where fictitious worlds arise from a voice.

Is the translator of literature a traitor as it says in Italian (traduttore-traditore) or an unfaithful mistress (une belle infidèle) or perhaps even a cannibal? I for my part believe in the metaphor of the translator as a musician that performs the text as a musical score. With a very important addition indeed, to which I shall return later.

My point of departure in this matter is an idea of the affinity between literary translation and working with literature in general. This affinity has also been noted in recent theories about translation, which seem to have shifted their focus from linguistic aspects to cultural and not least literary and text oriented reflections on translation, as described in Hanne Jansens survey of the state of arts in this volume. Cf. also Annette Lindegaard (1997) who discusses the influence from Derrida and Bakhtin on translation theory. My own interest in the subject is partly due to my teaching of and research in Italian literature, and partly to my activities as translator of primarily Italo Calvino and Gianni Celati into Danish.

I shall start out with discussing the importance of translating when working with literature. As a second step I shall turn the question upside down and investigate how literary theories about text and interpretation can shed light on translation.

Translation and the teaching of literature

Translating a literary text from a foreign language into your mother tongue takes you directly into its intimate core. A student reader of a literary work in a foreign language does not always master the language well enough, especially not in the beginning of his or her studies: he or she does not know enough words (e.g. does not know their meaning: neither the most simple denotative meaning nor the whole spectrum of the possible uses), he or she becomes caught up in complex syntactical structures, while the foreign language has not yet acquired personal and cultural connotations for the person in question: he or she is not yet able to make the foreign language function 'cognitively' – that is, to grasp and configure image schemes which also on an aesthetic level allow spaces of signification to unfold.

But if in the course of your studies, you decide to translate literature you inevitably develop these competences. In the process of translating, the foreign text is – in a questioning and pendular movement – confronted with your own language, which is rooted in your own experience of the world. This cognitive experience of language is, in the process of translation, embodied in the foreign text, which simultaneously presents its foreignness as a challenge to one's own linguistic experience. In trying to comprehend and then render the aesthetic form of the literary text you reach out for literature's singular ability to create meaning and to test and expand the potential expressiveness of language. Similarly, many authors translate other authors with the purpose of assimilating their linguistic aesthetics, much like a cannibal who assimilates the power of his own ancestor by devouring him.

The integration of literary translations in the teaching of literature makes it possible to *simultaneously* discuss the semantic, the cultural and the aesthetic in detail, because the students are confronted with the differences and with the foreignness of the text in a very direct experience. Unfortunately time is taken up by many other paramount aspects in the teaching of literature, and the close reading and the insight into the details of a text which the process of translating offers as a means to understanding the text are therefore seldom utilised. Oral translations are often too time-consuming, but written translations of short stories and text excerpts can successfully be discussed in relation to key words, the narrating voice, level of style e.g. In one of my courses, about fantastic literature in the 20.th century, the students each translated and commented on a short story. Three students corrected the translations and wrote introductions to the various writers, as a part of their final BA-exams. Eventually the book was published and met critical acclaim.

The "corporeality" of the text

Translating a text – as well as reading it aloud – creates a situation where one experiences the corporeality of the text: the sensuous aspects of meaning are woven together with the whole semantic field in a movement towards the configuration of the fictitious universe, raised by and imbedded in the sensuality of language, in its *voice*. This aspect of the text is mainly described in terms of sound: rhythm, timbre, tone, modulation. But not only are rhythm and sound activated in the inner ear of the reader, the inner eye opens up as well, to the visual properties of the text. Cognitive theories of language understand texts as organised in image schemes with important sensorial components (on image schemes and their not propositional but imaginistic character, v. Lakoff: 1987; 440-46).

It was recording for blind readers Italo Svevo's *La coscienza di Zeno* that inspired me to analyse the ironic voice in this novel. I immediately experienced the physical presence of the narrating voice, the tone and the obliquities of the ironic discourse which can be analysed (and experienced) in the horizontal perspective of the text's unpredictable progression. But very much also vertically, as levels, traps, drops in the text, that open the empty spaces of language under the reader.

Likewise it was the process of translating the works of Calvino, especially *Le città invisibili* and *Palomar,* that made me experience the visuality of the text so intensely that in my present project I have chosen to investigate the importance of visuality in Calvino's texts.

Literary theory, interpretation, translation
The light that textual analysis sheds on literary forms and thematic structures is essential to the understanding of literature and, as a consequence, also to translating. I wish however to focus here on the importance of theories of interpretation as a means to understanding the role and status of the translator and the translated text, especially in relation to the aesthetic dimensions.

An important shift of paradigm in literary theory is constituted by 'the hermeneutic turn' which took place during the 60'es, at the same time as structuralism resurfaced in the shape of Semiotics. Umberto Eco's avant-garde aesthetics in the famous *Opera Aperta* (1962) constitutes an early example of this turn. In *Opera Aperta* Eco challenges the structuralist notion of the closed system by defining the work as 'open' to the reader or interpreter. The actual process of interpretation and the role of the reader are, however, investigated much later by Eco in a semiotic perspective in *Lector in Fabula* (1979),and *I Limiti dell'Interpretazione* (1990).

In Germany the Konstanz School develops interesting theories about 'the aesthetics of reception', with Jauss' historical research into the reception of the literary work as a kind of new literary history (1966), and Iser's (1970) focus on the interaction of the single empirical reader with the text and its 'empty spaces'. In France primarily Sartre and then Barthes pay attention to the role of the reader in the process of the text's signification; Derrida's theories of the destabilising of meaning follow around 1967.

The philosophical origins of this interest in the reader are to be found in phenomenology where, in a kind of co-operation with earlier hermeneutic traditions, the work of art appears as given in the consciousness of the reader, the viewer or the listener, The Polish philosopher Roman Ingarden's theories of aesthetic cognition (Erkennen) are very important to this line of study. Although the various theories display some fundamental differences, especially the French and the German schools, some general tendencies appear to be common:

The ontological status of the literary work (text).
The idea of the work of art as a closed system with a finite meaning, which applies to both the Romantic notion of the original work of art and Structuralism has been substituted by an idea of the open work.
One true meaning versus many possible meanings.
The focus of literary interpretation is displaced from finding the true meaning of the text to grasping the text as a point of departure in a process of signification where meaning no longer is unequivocal.

From writer, genesis and system to reader and interpretation.
As a consequence the critical interest shifts its focus from the text as system or the genesis of the text (Biography, Marxism, Psychological Criticism) to the text as signification in a semiotic sense, or to the processes of interpretation in a hermeneutic sense.

The openness of the text appears in two different ways:
A) As part of a notion of a 'fluid' text (intertextuality) which implies that texts interact, that they are intrinsically interwoven in endless intertextual relations. According to this notion the meaning/signification is never enclosed in the text and never finite – it comes from other texts, it is formed in dialogical relationships with other texts and it continues in news texts (Kristeva, Derrida and partly Bachtin). This French tradition constitutes the basis of American Deconstruction.
B) As an openness in the text-reader relation: the text is understood as not concluded until the reader actualise the text by his configuration and interpretation (especially the hermeneutic school and in another perspective, Eco).

It is evident that the hermeneutic turn is relevant to our understanding of the act of translating. If the text no longer is an irreplaceable finite and original work of art – if the text no longer has one and only one true meaning – well, then translating will be much more satisfying. It will no longer be a question of striving for an impossible identity, it is not a matter of treachery or infidelity: the translation becomes one of the *forms* in which the text exists. I hesitate to say that it becomes one of its many *interpretations:* although the act of translation cannot be separated from the act of interpretation, the former ought not to be reduced to an interpretation. I will return to this point later.

Susan Bassnett (1991; 79) has a point when she says that concepts like translations, versions, adaptations have been discussed at length, trying to establish a hierarchy of 'correctness' between these categories: "Yet the differentiation between them derives from a concept of the reader as a passive receiver of the text in which Truth is enshrined. In other words, if the text is perceived as an object that should only produce a single invariant reading, any 'deviation' on the part of the reader/translator will be judged as a transgression." And later: "One of the greatest advances in twentieth century literary studies has been the re-evaluation of the reader." Bassnett mentions Barthes' understanding of the reader as "producer of texts, while Kristeva sees the reader as realizing the expansion of the work's process of semiosis". And concludes, with Octavio Paz, that "all texts are translations of translations of translations and the lines cannot be drawn to separate Reader from Translator."

Translation as deconstructing the notion of 'literary work'
Italo Calvino's *Se una notte d'inverno un viaggiatore* is probably the first novel in which translations contribute to the deconstruction of the notion of 'work' in literature. The book consists in ten beginnings, embedded in a frame story in eleven chapters. In the frame story readers, writers, translators and critics write, read, discuss, and misplace – the various beginnings. These are not ten different novels but rather the same story displaced and metamorphosed through ten different genre pastiches. One of the reasons for this gradual dissolution of the idea of the one original novel and its replacement by an idea of the perpetually mutable text is the presence of the translator Hermes Marana (Hermes: God of theft, transience, exchange). His activities as a translator consist in falsifications, exchanges, and not least translations of non-existent originals. It is – as the book's many readers can testify – an extremely funny deconstruction of literary and critical positions, a kind of very precise sociology of literature and at the same time a narrative about the joys of literature with archetypical themes. The result is a 'real' book, which even in its Danish translation has become a cult book in literary circles.

That means, once again, you can very well deconstruct the work, but you have to translate the text anyway! And it works. And you can very well argue that in a broad sense all texts are translations of something else, and that therefore Translation is impossible (cf. the discussion in Hanne Jansen (2002) of linguistic and postmodern untranslatability). But in the final analysis you could also claim the opposite: We have seen that the idea of the one true meaning makes translation equally impossible. Maybe both understandings in their extreme make translation impossible. But I insist on claiming a point in between these two extreme positions where translation in a strict sense is possible, necessary, and essential, with its own ethics. In my opinion the hermeneutic approach offers a very fertile perspective on the affinity between theories of translation and theories of reading and interpretation. And it is more important to understand the implications of this affinity than to walk the deconstructive plank.

The double interpretation

Both French-American deconstruction and German hermeneutics have contributed to the dissolution of the notion of the work and the idea of the one true meaning. But their contributions to the understanding of literary translations differ widely. The 'horizontal' displacement of meaning through texts in Derrida-inspired deconstruction offers a paramount philosophical frame for a discussion of the destabilisation of meaning. But not, as far as I can see, a point of departure in relation to the aesthetic aspects of literary translation.

The hermeneutic approach seems a greater inspiration, especially in regard to an idea about a double interpretation or reading. There are two objects of interest in the phenomenologically inspired approach to art: 1) the form and structure of the work of art, and 2) the work (or text) as it is realised in the experience of an actual reader or viewer. After all, the text comes into existence only in the moment it is performed by a reader. The hermeneutic position, says Iser (2000) opens up a space between the text to be interpreted and the interpreter. In this space the meaning of the text oscillates between the authority of the text and the authority of the reading. Hermeneutics is a negotiation of this space and the interpretation is therefore not an explanation but an action, a performance.

These two fields of interest in the process of interpretation can be described in different ways. Ingarden distinguishes 1) the stratified structure of the literary work (the form) as opposed to 2) the modality of actualisation (Konkretisierung), which is the reader's experience of the work. To achieve cognition of the first field it is necessary to describe structures, possibly without interpretation. The notion of actualisation is very important: the text does not appear in its 'concrete' corporeal form before it is experienced by a reader.

Wolfgang Iser (1978) says that the literary work consists of two poles, the artistic pole (the text created by the artist) and the aesthetic pole, the actualisation or ideation formed by the reader. The literary work is not to be situated in either of the poles, but where they meet. "The work is the coming into presence of the text in the reader's consciousness". In a later article (Iser 79) he divides the interpretational work in *interpretation* which aims at establishing the semantic significance, and *reception*, which is the production of the aestetic object by the reader according to the structural and functional schemes inherent in the text.

Umberto Eco (1990; 29) also speaks of two levels of interpretation, but in a different way: 1) what he calls the *semantic interpretation* is seen as the result of the process whereby the reader fills the linear manifestation of the text with meaning. He also calls this process a naive reading, because the reader lets himself be trapped by the ruses of the text; 2) *the critical* or *semiotical interpretation* aims at explaining the structural reasons why the text produces this and other semantic interpretations. So in his two levels Eco does not include the aesthetic dimension, and seems therefore to exclude the cognitive experience of the sensory forms.

In *Lector in fabula* Eco has a short discussion of a translation, where he argues that the translation necessarily represents a closing of the open spaces of the text:

> La traduzione è corretta, ma come vedremo "aggiunge" qualcosa al testo originale: cioè colloca sotto forma di lessemi nella superficie lineare del testo ciò che l'originale inglese lasciava all'attualizzazzione del lettore, procedimento tipico di tutte le traduzioni, le quali infatti rappresentano, quando sono riuscite, un esempio di cooperazione interpretativa messo in pubblico (…) Il traduttore è un lettore empirico che si è comportato come un lettore modello. (Eco: 1979; 188)

– and in my translation:

> The translation is correct, but as we shall see, it "adds" something to the original text: it places in the linear surface of the text as lexemes what the English original left to the actualisation of the reader; this is a typical procedure for all translations, as they represent, when successfully done, an example of an interpretative cooperation made public (…) The translator is an empirical reader who acts as a model reader.

This position seems to me a reductive understanding of the literary translation process.

In Collins, *The reading of the written image* (1991, es. pp.101-131) I have found an interesting theoretical discussion of the process of interpretation in relation to literary text. Collins is inspired both by hermeneutics and semiotics (Peirce). He critizes Eco for having skipped a mental, psychological dimension in Peirce's concept of the Interpretant in order to maintain publicly coded signification as the only field for semiotic studies.

What is illuminating in Collin's theories is the fact that he divides each act of interpretation in two parts: 1) a private construction of understanding and 2) a public presentation of this understanding. The musician's interpretational work can be divided into the private rehearsals and the public performance (the concert); while the problem concerning the reader's performance of the literary work lies in the fact that it is internally cued; it is silent and thus not subject to control. It is therefore impossible to distinguish between on one hand the "skilfully produced silent performances", which Collins calls *enactive interpretations* and on the other hand bad, imprecise, arbitrary performances, which we could with Eco call uses of the text. For this reason we need *critical interpretations*, which explain and reflect the quality of the encounter with the text. The enactive interpretation has low priority in the discourse on literature, while the critical approach has been triumphant, because it can be verified and therefore is attractive in pedagogical praxis. The *enactive interpretation* is a performance of the text, but relies also on a critical-analytical dimension to acquire quality. "Interpretation is an activity that emcompasses two distinct but independent procedures, immediate construal and mediate exegesis."

The translator and the double process of translation

Where is the translator situated in this process? That all translation is an act of interpretation, is true in the sense that the process of translation begins with a reading necessarily consisting in an interpretation. This first interpretation is a performative interpretation, that is a performance of the text, combined with more or less explicited analytical approaches.

However, when we consider the second process in the interpretation, the moment of its becoming "public", the idea of the interpretation as both 1) a twofold process consisting in a private and a public moment, and 2) a double relation to the text (a performative and an analytical) allows us to give a more precise account of the translator's role and goals, and the status of the translated text: in the first process the reader "performs" the text to himself, while in the second process there should be no direct transfer of this performance to a new language; that is not possible in an hermeneutic perspective. What is possible, is to produce a text – in close interplay with and governed by the performative interpretation – that can function as a new musical score o the readers in the new language, and enable them to form – equivalent – enactive interpretations.

For this reason it is only partly true to see the translator as a musician performing the text. The translator can not offer the whole of his performance to the new reader, as can the musician; and he should not try to produce a too interpretative text, or – as Eco puts it – a semantic interpretation, that is the filling-in reading of the model reader.

Naturally, I am fully aware that because of the linguistic and semantic differences between the languages, and because of the openness and ambivalences inherent in the literary text, and finally because the new text is "governed" by an enactive interpretation – it will be absolutely impossible not to encounter in the new "score" many elements of "interpretation" in the sense of "explication" of the original text . But these elements are often too many. In my opinion it is very important to stress, that it is not the interpretation of the text, but its "virtual presence" in its openness that is to be transferred.

In a literary perspective it does not sound very reassuring that there should exist ""translation universals" i.e. linguistic properties which characterize translation (...) such as explication, simplification, levelling-out and conventionalization" (quoted from Hanne Jansen 2002; 130). It seems to be connected with the concept of "adaptation", which I would consider a wrong ideal for a normal modern literary translation process.

Cf. in this respect the illuminating analysis (Boisen 1996) of the French translation of the Danish novel "Smilla's Sense of Snow". It clearly shows the French translator's adaptation of the often very innovative Danish language into a standard literary-academic French. Eric Jacobsen (1994), in an interesting article on the traditions of translation in a historical perspective, mentions the medieval tradition for combining translations and commentaries, a method to which – in my opinion – the concept of adaptation has a certain affinity.

I would rather agree with Stolze (2001, as quoted by Hanne Jansen 2002; 128): "There is no such thing as a "transfer", but the cognitive representation of the message links the translation to the original (…); translation is a matter of writing (so to create 'presence' for the original message), not so much of intercultural comparison". That does not imply, of course, that cultural competence does not hold – as mentioned above, and discussed in the article by Ingemai Larsen in this volume – a very important place as a condition for "creating presence" in another language. Neither does it imply that there is no transfer of culture when literary texts are translated. But it does imply that instead of stressing the process of mediation or adaptation, we should stress an understanding of the literary translation as creating a sort of aesthetic-hermeneutical equivalence, in the sense of equivalent possibilities for the new reader to experience the openness of the text and create his own performance.

A recent example in Denmark of a discussion of open and closed translations is to be found in a fine short article by the Danish writer and translator Niels Brunse (2001) on two translations into Danish of Kafka's novel *The Castle*, the first one by the writer H. C.Branner (1949) and the second by the writer, critic and philosopher Villy Sørensen. "Villy Sørensen has given us a new translation of Kafka with room for interpretation", says Brunse, underlining the fact that the many and very different critical interpretations of Kafka's novel over the years, show how important it is that a translator should not create obstructions by allowing his own interpretation to close the openness of the text. The translation of Branner adds Christian connotations, as when the German "mit stummer Bitte" is translated into "med stum bøn om tilgivelse" (with a mute prayer for forgiveness); while Villy Sørensen, who has also as a critic occupied himself with Kafka, retains the possibilities of interpretation in Kafka's "simple and yet enigmatic language." The translation of Villy Sørensen builds on an understanding of the text, that stresses the necessity to transfer the enigmas of the text.

This example allows us also to consider, what should not be forgotten: that the good literary translation relies very much on consistent – if not wholly explicited – critical interpretations, which illuminate the more immediate

Literary Translations between Philology and Aesthetics 147

and ongoing tentatives of performance. As Collins puts it (1991; 104) concerning the interpretation of literary texts in general: "A critical interpretation is only as informative as its enactive interpretation was skillful; and enactive interpretation is only as skillful as its critical interpretation was informed;" this holds true also for the translation.

Certain elements of the text can best – or only – be grasped in the sensory experience of the text: it would be qualities like rhythm, sounds, modalities of tone and colour of the voices of the text, especially the narrating voice; it would be the visuality of the descriptions and the metaphors. Other elements are more easily analyzed or explicited in a critical dimension, as for instance thematic words (and the semantic conflicts which occur in this field while translating), narrative structures (the use of the person-category connected with narrators (first, third person) or readers). Too little attention to those – and other similar – structures can be seen in many translations. You encounter them for instance, when you try to use translations to illustrate problems of this kind.

In my opinion it is important – also pedagogically – to distinguish these two parts with their different demands, in the process of interpretation and translation. But as the interplay between sensory qualities and signification of the form *and* the semantics of the language is a the very core of the literary text and the literary experience, in reality the two parts can not be seperated; both ways of creating cognition interfere constantly with each other in the ongoing process of translating.

The fundamental interplay between the aesthetic and the semantic performance or interpretation of the text

I would like to conclude with a few examples in order to shed light on the interplay between a dominantly sensory modality of the reading, and a more semantic approach. Developing this part would demand much more space, and I would encounter the difficulty of discussing in English translations into Danish of the Italian novels by Calvino and Celati.

I would however just like to point out, with three very short examples, this interaction of for instance visibility and tone with semantics. The translation of texts characterized by marked visual qualities, as are Calvino's texts, requires an attention both to the quality (the space aspects) of the images which the reader-translator sees with his mind's eye (forms, colours, lines, texture, glimpses of light, ecc.) and to the development of the image in the text (the time aspect): the order in which it unfolds itself in the linearity of the text. Translating the image requires a constant control in the modality of the enactive interpretation to secure 1) that the new text does create an image when read, and 2) that this image has the same or equivalent elements and effects as in the original text. It is easy to weaken the visual qualities even in a good "semantic" translation. A very short example of this problem is found in the danish translation (1961) of *Il cavaliere inesistente* (1959) of Calvino. Calvino himself tells us that the idea of the book came to him as the image of a knight, who consisted only of a void armour. And when the text begins the description of the knight – in order, I would argue, to present to our mind's eye this image – it says: "..un cavaliere dall'armatura tutta bianca; solo una ringhina nera correva torno torno ai bordi ;..." (Calvino 1991; 957) that is, first we have the colour of the armour (shining white), and then the next words draw the outlines of what I see as a graphic image of the knight: (only a thin black line ran...). The Danish tranlation has for the last phrase: " kun en tynd linie af sort..." (only a thin line of black); and in my opinion and experience the change of position of 'black' from an epithet to 'line' to a prepositional syntagma makes it difficult for the reader to visualize the graphic image.

The rhythm and the sound of the words are other sensous parts of the text, important to the quality of the voice which you experience – physically, in a sensory mode – in the reading of a literary text. In Calvino the rhythm is of great relevance, both the overall, almost classical rhythm of the structure of the text, and the more specific – often comic – effects of creating climaxes in the many catalogue-like descriptions or narrations.

The close relationship in literary translation between the semantic part and the sensory mode can be discussed briefly in the translation of titles. Calvinos *Le città invisibili* structures the 55 descriptions of cities, set in a frame of Marco Polos relations to The Great Khan – in eleven groups which have important thematic titles. The group of cities called "le città sottili" presents a semantic problem for translation into Danish (and English). "Sottile" in Italian means both a physical quality (thin, "magro" –) and a transposed meaning of mental qualities: (subtle). The English translation has chosen to focus on the first part, speaking of a category of "thin cities". It might have been just possibile to use "subtle" for both, but "subtle cities" has a very ugly and unpoetic sound. In Danish I could not have chosen "tynde byer": it sounds almost hilarious, due both to the sound of the vowels and the semantics of the words put together. "Spinkle byer" might well have been possible, but I did not think that "spinkel" had the semantic potential to suggest the utopian qualities of this group of cities. So I turned to the other meaning, the mental qualities, and called the category "Underfundige byer".

Celatis *Narratori delle pianure* (Voices from the Plain) is composed by 30 small stories, all having thematic key-word titles, often difficult to translate. The beautiful and terrible last story is entitled "Giovani umani in fuga". It is almost untranslatable into Danish, because of the substantivation of 'umani' as 'exemplars of the human species' (not common in Italian, and impossible in Danish). It conveys in Italian a picture of a plain (la pianura) were your eyes follow a small troop of young 'humans', almost like antelopes, trying to escape fear and violence. It is a perfect title in Italian: visual and suggestive as the title of a painting, and very difficult not to banalize to simple "explanation" in Danish (Unge på flugt/ Unge mennesker på flugt).

In these examples – and in literary translation as a whole – you cannot separate the philological approch from the aesthetic.

References:
Bassnett, Susan: 1991 (1980). *Translation Studies*. London-New York, Routledge.
Boisen, Jørn: 1996. *Mademoiselle Smilla. Overvejelser over en oversættelse.* NOK 111, Odense Universitetsforlag.
Brunse, Niels: 2001. "Slottet istandsat". *Politiken,* 10.3.
Calvino, Italo : 1991. *Romanzi e racconti.* Vol. I. Milano, Mondadori.
Collins, Christhopher: 1991. *Reading The Written Image*. Pennsylvania State University Press.
Eco, Umberto: 1979. *Lector in fabula.* Milano, Bompiani.
Eco, Umberto: 1990.*I limiti dell'interpretazione.* Milano.
Iser, Wolfgang: 1978. *The Act of Reading*, (orig 1976. *Der Akt des Lesens*)
Iser, Wolfgang: 1989. "Il processo della letteratura. Una prospettiva fenomonologica." *Teoria della ricezione,* a cura di Robert C. Holub, Torino, Eianudi, pp. 259-284. (orig. "The Current Situation of Literary Theory: Key Concepts and the Imaginary." *New Literary History,* VXI (1979), pp. 1-20)
Iser, Wolfgang: 2000. *The Range of Interpretation*. New York, Columbia University Press.
Jansen, Hanne: (2002). "Translation Studies: From Linguistics and Beyond and Back again". (In this volume).
Lakoff, George: 1987. *Women, Fire and Dangerous Things*. Chicago, University of Chicago Press.
Lindegaard, Annette: (1997). "Translation, Deconstruction and Dialogism". Dollerup et al. (red.): *An Introduction to Translation Studies.* København, Center for oversættelsesvidenskab, pp. 69-82.

Translation and Cultural History

by

Ingemai Larsen

University of Copenhagen

As stated by Hanne Jansen in the previous article, what happens in the translation process is the *meeting* of two cultures, or their *confrontation*. Whichever expression one chooses – and each evokes quite different associations – it functions as a reminder that translation must be regarded as cultural transmission of the most concrete and tangible type, and should thus be undertaken with great conscientiousness. A translation is never transparent: it is based on a number of choices, and always comes with a history of its reception reflecting to a greater or lesser extent the intentions of its writer.

In this article I intend to deal with the relationship between cultural history and translation practice with reference to the problems that arise when working with texts in a minor language[1] and with texts written in a postcolonial context. My aim is not to suggest solutions to the various problems connected to the translation of these types of texts but to demonstrate the importance of cultural history, and the intimate relation between this knowledge and an understanding of the text's linguistic and literary dimensions. Thus I hope to make clear how conducive a total environment of language studies can be to the craft of translation.

Whilst working with texts from minor language areas is presumably of relevance to all Language Studies Departments, this is not necessarily the case with postcolonial texts. As regards the Department of Romance Languages in Copenhagen, our field of study obliges us to deal with both types of text, and in the case of my own discipline, Portuguese Studies, on a rather large scale. A student of Portuguese is likely to encounter texts both from so-called "young" postcolonial nations, such as East Timor,

---

[1] Quoting Lawrence Venuti, I understand *minority* to "mean a cultural or political position that is subordinate, whether the social context that so defines it is local, national or global" (Venuti 1998; 1).

Mozambique and Angola, from an "old" postcolonial nation, Brazil[2], and from minor language areas, for instance the partly Creole speaking Cape Verde, which is at the same time a former colony.

Two clarifying remarks: First: Like most translators I maintain the pragmatic attitude that texts in general as well as postcolonial texts and minor language texts are translatable; with loss, however, that *may* be considerable when focusing specifically on these two types. Thus the ideal of equivalence stands a severe test if we rely on the consensual definition maintaining that the TL-reader and the SL-reader must share the same experience and message when they meet or are confronted with a given text for the first time. However, one way of reducing the loss is to take into account as many details as possible of the historical and cultural context of the text.

And second: When I talk about historical and cultural context/cultural history, it must be understood that I use an umbrella designation covering a multiplicity of subcategories of histories: of literature, of politics, of language, of society, and also of the history of concepts, which in the context of Language Studies I find it particularly relevant to draw attention to. As described by, for instance, Reinhard Kosellech, this branch of historiography offers a sensitive understanding of the sediments of the cultural history of a nation or a region as it works across three disciplinary domains: the linguistic (semantic) dimension; the performative (social) dimension; and the chronological (historical) dimension, tracing the development of a given concept as a guideline through history. Despite not having carried out any detailed investigation into the relationship between the two areas of study (and with the supposition that it has not been done by anyone else) I see obvious - though partial - parallels between the methodology of the historian of concepts and that of the translator. The historian is aware in his work that a concept transcends the historically specific word, picking up semantic content in concentrated forms, and thus exists in a tension between the socio-historical context and the actual word. This double perspective also underlies the work of the translator, and in a wider sense of a Department of Language Studies: words cannot be translated or analyzed if separated from their social, cultural and

---

[2] In this connection I do not intent to problematize the definition of "postcolonial" (although it is perfectly possible to do so when referring to the Portuguese ex-empire) – but simply use the term as a synonym for former colonized nations. What matters in this context is that, as a rule, the Portuguese language used in Brazil differs from that of the former African colonies, which is different again from the continental standardized Portuguese. Thus the different usages of the three continents present as many challenges for the translator.

historical setting: these two dimensions, in fact, mutually constitute and reflect one another.

For the historian of concepts working on the periphery of Linguistics, it is the concept which is the key to understanding, and the objection may be raised that this is only part of the work of the translator. However, the dialectical relation between language and the extra-linguistic world operates in and has been formulated by all branches of the Humanities.

Susan Bassnett has put it very precisely in a connection pointing towards the postcolonial problematic on which I will comment below:

> The problems of decoding a text for a translator involve so much more than language, despite the fact that the basis of any written text *is* its language. Moreover, the importance of understanding what happens in the translation process lies at the heart of our understanding of the world we inhabit. And if translation studies have been increasingly concerned with the relationship between individual texts and the wider cultural system within which those texts are produced and read, it is therefore not surprising that within cultural studies, and in post-colonial theory in particular, translation is increasingly being seen both as actual practice and as metaphor. (Bassnett 1998; 137)

In concrete terms, this means that in the translation process the choices we make regarding the text's register on the basis of the decoding of the text are, in fact, socio-linguistically defined choices, which Mona Baker has described in this way:

> Register variation arises from variation in the following:
> **Field** *of discourse*: (...) Different linguistic choices are made by different speakers depending on what kind of action other that the immediate action of speaking they see themselves as participating in. For example (...) a football match or discussing football; making love or discussing love; making a political speech or discussing politics (...)
> **Tenor** *of discourse*: (...) the language people use varies depending on interpersonal relationship as mother/child, doctor/patient, or superior/inferior in status (...)
> **Mode** *of discourse*: An abstract term for the role that the language is playing (speech, essay, lecture, instructions) and for its medium of transmission (spoken, written). (Baker: 1992; 15-16)

Since these are all socio-linguistic choices, they all draw to a greater or lesser degree on knowledge of the culture (where is the football match taking place and what linguistic consequences has this? what level of politeness is required in Portugal in a conversation between mother and child in a lower middle-class family? etc.) Thus expanding our synchronic and diachronic analysis in order to identify the context as a whole is an ongoing process.

The first question asked is *when?* But the whole range of conditions surrounding this *when* are also inquired into: for instance, the circumstances in which a given text was produced, the history of its reception and the extent to which this history corresponds to the intention of the writer, as far as this can be known.

In the following examples I will concentrate on these aspects of the decoding of the text, leaving implicit the consideration of their interrelation with linguistic and literary aspects.

Ela cantou um fado [She sang a fado] serves an example of the interdependence between the utterance/text and the context. If instead of including *fado* as a loan word and thus retaining its expressive and associative content (which in fact seems a good option) the translator chooses to make use of a descriptive paraphrase, the historical and cultural context of *fado* would have to be considered. In this case the history of reception would be particularly relevant. Possible translations include:

1) She sang an emotional traditional folksong
2) She sang a nationalistic glorifying song

1) is likely to be the most common translation where the intention of the original is to produce a neutral text (such as an Encyclopedia entry); whereas
2) might well have been used to translate a text from the 1980s, when Amália, the great interpreter of *fado,* was associated with the fascist Salazar regime and the fado-texts became objects of ideological criticism.

Another illustration of the interdependency between historical period and semantic content is the concept *católico militante,* referring to an active, even propagandistic, Catholic in 1920s Portugal, a kind of missionary in his own country (bearing witness to the fact that in the previous decade the church had been completely deprived of its power). Again, depending on the context and the evaluation of the writer's intention of naming himself or another as literally a *militant Catholic,* the translator may consider whether to give the concept positive or negative associations in the TL-text.

We may also regard the discourse on the nation as an obvious place to track down the sediments deposited through cultural history and the historical development of concepts. With regard to texts from 20th-century Portugal, national discourse will often be found to be penetrated by religious, metaphysical terminology, and although this characteristic is most prominent in slightly older texts it is also noticeable in texts of more recent date, whether political writing, literary works or essays. Roughly speaking, this can be explained by the comparatively very late secularization of the concept of nationality, which again is due to the use made in the 20th century of a strongly mythologized nationalistic discourse by a dictatorship that lasted for almost 50 years.

An unreflective translation of, for instance, an editorial written in connection with *Expo/98*, the World Exhibition in Lisbon, might well seem pathetic. The editorial declares that the exhibition markes "a grande viagem ao futuro pontuada de sonho e utopia. Uma festa em que Portugal e o mundo se reencontra" [a grand voyage to the future, punctuated by dream and utopia. A celebration in which Portugal and the world reencounter each other] (Jornal do Fundão, 1998; 1). However, in the remainder of the article it is repeatedly stressed that Portugal is finally being released from her unrealistic self-image. A translation based on a knowledge of the historical and cultural context detailed above would probably maintain a strategy in which considerations of the intentions of the text as a whole were balanced against the contradictory associations of the stylistic level and some of the terminology.

But how is it to be understood when José Saramago, the Portuguese Nobel Prize winner, uses the same discourse in his novels? Here the pathetic ought probably to be stressed. In this connection choices will be made on the basis of the translator's knowledge of the chapters of political and cultural history mentioned above, of the use and abuse of the myths of Portugal, of the history of Portuguese literature, and of the life and works of the writer. So when in *O Ano da Morte de Ricardo Reis/The Year of the Death of Ricardo Reis* Saramago informs us that in 1936 Portugal is celebrating because of

> o aparecimento do professor António de Oliveira Salazar na vida pública, há oito anos, parece que ainda foi ontem, como o tempo passa, para salvar o seu e o nosso pais do abismo, para o restaurar, para lhe impor uma nova doutrina, fé, entusiasmo e confiança no futuro [the appearance of Professor António de Oliveira Salazar in public life, eight years ago, it seems that it was just yesterday, see how time flies, to save his and our country from the abyss, to restore faith, enthusiasm and trust in the future by imposing on it [the country] a new doctrine]. (Saramago 1984; 298)

we are confident that the translation must be close to the literal, and this confidence is supported by our identification of the textual mode as ironic.

As my examples make clear, I am moving towards a consideration of cultural *confrontations*, towards the types of texts in which, calculatedly and for particular reasons, certain linguistic strategies are integrated. The ethical considerations demanded in any translation process may seem even more pressing when working with minor language text and postcolonial texts, because aspects such as unequal power relations and attempts to destabilize the dominating forms of representation are actualised.

Within translation studies it is common to say that the target language is, by definition, "poorer" than the source language, and to regard this as demonstrating that there is never complete correspondence between the languages and cultures of two nations/regions etc. However, when translating texts from former colonies one must be aware that in the author's point of view the relationship between the regional language and in particular European languages may be far from equal. For many postcolonial writers, the egalitarian conception of languages (all source languages are equally rich) maintained by translation studies is an ideal not borne out in actual practice.

This has historical grounds which almost always involve accounts of the suppression of language and culture, and of the inhabitants of the colony lacking education and access to the language that conferred and still confers influence; and also of a literature that did not achieve the conditions in which it could develop on its own terms until very recently.

Texts from former colonies, however, are rarely written in a regional language; most commonly they use the language of the old colonial power, often – which I will be commenting on further – in a transformed version. This does not simplify matters.

In relation to minor languages, the core of the problem also concerns asymmetrical power relations. Following Lawrence Venuti, I understand a minor language both as the language of a politically dominated group and also as a language *use* that deviates from the standard (Venuti: 1998; 2). Venuti refers to an example from a German context taken from Deleuze and Guattari:

> In the Austrian Empire Czech was a minor language in relation to German; but the German of Prague already functioned as a potentially minor language in relation to the German of Vienna or Berlin; and Kafka, a Czechoslovakian Jew writing in German, submits German to creative treatment as a minor language, constructing a continuum of variation. (Deleuze & Guattari 1987; 3)

In many former colonies, such as the former Portuguese colonies in Africa, the situation is similar to the one described in the quotation (which in fact refers to a European "colonial" problematic). In countries like Mozambique and Angola, the regional languages are minor languages in relation to Portuguese, the official language, but at the same time the Portuguese spoken by the vast majority of the population (outside an elite of city dwellers) is a minor language in relation to continental Portuguese, since in terms of grammar and pronunciation it differs from the European standard. In this way the minor language text and the postcolonial text overlap. However, at the same time – cf. Kafka, mentioned in the quotation – various writers attempt to give a higher status to everyday colloquial Portuguese, a language subject to rapid development and transformation both because it is learnt in a local context parallel with many regional languages and because it is not taught on systematic educational principles. It should be added that for most of the population the teaching of Portuguese was only introduced within the last 25 years; until these nations gained independence in 1975, this was a privilege extended to a tiny minority.

The (language related) power struggles taking place in these countries leave very visible traces in the literature, and the translator will thus need to be familiar with:

- the power relations subsisting between the major and the minor languages/between the language of the colonial power and the regional language;
- the status of the minor language present and past /the regional language during and after independence;
- the reasons for the major language /the language of the colonizing power becoming the official language and the extent to which it is spoken by the population.

The complex of answers to these questions forms the basis of each writer's position in terms of language and self-conception and of his contribution to the construction of the collective language-defined identity.

Very often a pronounced ambivalence will appear in relation to the problematic that the language of the writer, whether imposed upon him or learnt at the expense of a regional language, does not correspond to the "authentic" language of his culture - no matter how dubious this polarization between authenticity and artificiality may be. What matters is that the purpose of the strategies of transformation which many postcolonial writers mobilize within the text, in the shape of deviations from orthographic, syntactic or morphological standards, is to articulate an independent and authentic identity. Concerning this problematic in an African context, Adejunmobi has pointed out that:

> In the larger context of preoccupations among African writers and critics, this conception can be related to another requirement, namely that the Africanness of any given European-language text be deduced not from the nationality of the author, but from specific strategies mobilized within the text. Such strategies include modeling European-language texts on African narratives and recreating a certain vision of African life in these texts. (Adejunmobi, 1998; 168)

Adejunmobi has identified three categories of texts and strategies, and his empirical material proves in no uncertain manner how manifest the ambivalence to the European languages is. The three categories are:

- a category (from the point of view of the translator the most straightforward) in which the writer's primary objective is to reach the widest possible audience. In this type of text, loan words from a regional language are not meant to signal cultural or ethnical authenticity, but are fully integrated.
- a diametrically opposite category of text is that which seeks to naturalize and thus manipulate the European language, indigenize it, so to speak. In this case the author of the text strives to make visible and to incorporate all the syntactic, stylistic and grammatical differences between the regional language and the European language in which he has chosen to write and from which the translation will be carried out.
- a last category comprising texts which, whilst they are based on markedly local materials such as songs, rhymes and narratives and thereby signal ethnicity, at the same time appear transparent because the writer has given priority to fluency rather than to "etnicity".

An example of a text that explicitly challenges the hegemony of language is the Angolan writer Luandino Vieira´s *Luuanda* from 1964, which holds an exceptional position in the history of Portuguese literature, culture and politics. In 1965, when Vieira was imprisoned at the instigation of the Portuguese authorities on a charge of "terrorist activity", he was awarded the *Grande Prémio* of the Portuguese Association of Writers for this collection of stories, and for this the Government ordered the abolition of the Association. It is hard to imagine a clearer manifestation of how language represents power.

> Dizia Xico Futa: Pode mesmo a gente saber, com a certeza, como é um caso começou, aonde começou, porquê, praquê, quem? Saber mesmo o que estava se passar no coração da pessoa que faz, que procura, desfaz ou estraga as conversas, as macas. Ou tudo o que na vida não pode-se-lhe agarrar no princípio e era também um fim doutro princípio e então, se a gente segue assim, para trás ou para frente, vê que não se pode partir o fio da vida, mesmo que está podre nalgum lado, ele sempre se emenda noutro sítio, cresce, desvia, foge, avança, curva, pára, esconde, aparece....E digo isto, tenho minha razão (Vieira1981; 69-70). [Xico Futa said: Can people really know for sure how something started, where it started, why, who for, who by? Really know what was going on in the heart of the person who starts confusions, looks for them, or undoes or ruins conversations? Or is it impossible to grasp the beginning of things in life, when you get to that beginning you see after all the same beginning was also the end of another beginning and then, if you go on like this, backwards and forwards, you see that the thread of life can´t be broken, even if it´s rotten at one point it always mends itself at another, it grows, it strays, flees, advances, turns, stops, disappears, appears... And I´ll say this, I know what I´m saying]. (Vieira, 1980, 43)

The English translation is far from doing full justice to the original text[3], whose extremely non-orthodox appearance is due to both Vieira's mixture of colloquial language and invented words and constructions and his "rattling" style. In terms of syntax the text presents various deviations from the standard (such as the placing of *mesmo* and the play with *pode-se-lhe*); it omits the definite article and deviates from standard rules for opening paragraphs (*Ou*), and none of these linguistic violations have been rendered in the translation. Another deviant feature concealed by the translation is the break with standard Portuguese orthography (*praquê*).

So all in all, the translation reads far more fluently than the original, is far more consistent with standard norms of grammar and syntax, and strikes one as being on an altogether different stylistic level.

The linguistic hybridism present in this type of text may be the product of artistic creativity, or primarily a political-ideological project, or, as is the case with Luandino Vieira's writings, a mixture of the two. Depending on the degree to which the translator respects the non-standard formulations and inventions, the TL text will contribute to a change in the major language and thus, ultimately, change the existing power relation between SL and TL.

It goes without saying that to be able to respect the writer's intention it is extremely important for the translator to consider such a text in the relevant historical and cultural setting. Precisely the question of intention constitutes in this respect the crux of the matter. Not all translators have the same privileged working conditions as those of Gunter Grass (who meet with their author whenever a new book of his is released[4]); the more the reason for them to strive for adequate knowledge and understanding.

As has been demonstrated, proficiency in the history of culture extends from information about morphology and syntax at the one extreme by way of knowledge of the distinctive features of literary genres to understanding the general traits of world history at the other extreme. A tall order, and obviously an ideal.

This returns me to the opening of the article, since to attain this ideal is exactly the ambition of a Department of Language Studies. The multidisciplinary approach, stressing both the linguistic, literary and historical-cultural dimensions as described in the three articles of this section, is the distinguishing feature of our Language Studies. A very significant *raison d'être* of ours is to contribute to enabling meetings and confrontations

---

[3] In reality the translators, Tamara Bender and Donna Hill, did not have a fair chance to do otherwise. My comments are not be interpreted as negative criticism of the translation.

[4] Cf. Øhrgaard, 2002.

between different cultures: in building bridges between past and future, time and place, the translation process has an important role to play.

References

Adejunmobi, Moradewun: 1998. "Translation and Postcolonial Identity - African Writing and European Languages". Venuti (ed.): 1998. *The Translator*, vol. 4, 2. Manchester, St. Jerome Publishing.

Baker, Mona: 1992. *In Other Words*. London-New York, Routledge.

Bassnett, Susan: 1998. "The Translation Turn in Cultural Studies". Bassnett and Lefevre: 1998. *Constructing Cultures – Essays on Literary Translation*. Clevedon, Multilingual Matters.

Deleuze & Guattari: 1987. "A Thousand Plateaus", cit. in Venuti:1998. *The Translator*, vol. 4, 2. Manchester, St. Jerome Publishing.

Jornal do Fundão: 1998 (22.5). Fundão.

Kosellech, Reinhard: 1989. *Vergangene Zukunft. Zur Semantik geschichtlicher Zeiten*. Frankfurt a/M, Suhrkamp.

Saramago, Jose: 1984. *O Ano da Morte de Ricardo Reis*. Lisboa, Caminho.

Venuti, Lawrence: 1998. "Introduction". *The translator*, vol. 4, 2. Manchester, St. Jerome Publishing.

Vieira, José Luandino: 1981. *Luuanda*. Lisboa, Edições 70.

Vieira, José Luandino: 1980. *Luuanda*, translated by Tamara Bender with Donna Hill. London, Heinemann.

Øhrgaard, Per: 2002. "Günter Grass og hans oversættere. En kort og ufuldstændig beretning om en hjemmeindustri" [Günter Grass and his translators. A short and incomplete account of a cottage industry] Anne-Sofie Didriksen (ed.): 2002. *Selv med døde fluer – en bog om Günter Grass* [Even with dead flies: a book about Günter Grass]. Århus, Aarhus Universitetsforlag.